WAR CRIMES IN GAZA AND THE ZIONIST FIFTH COLUMN IN AMERICA

WAR CRIMES IN GAZA

AND THE

ZIONIST FIFTH COLUMN IN AMERICA

JAMES PETRAS

CLEAR DAY BOOKS

ISBN: 0-9845255-0-5
     978-0-9845255-0-8

In-house editor: Diana G. Collier
Cover: R. Jordan P. Santos
Cover photo: AP/ Adel Hana

CLEAR DAY BOOKS
A subdivision of
Clarity Press, Inc.
Ste. 469, 3277 Roswell Rd. NE
Atlanta, GA. 30305 , USA
http://www.claritypress.com

To the Global BDS Movement
Boycott, Divestment and Sanctions for Palestine
http://bdsmovement.net/

TABLE OF CONTENTS

PREFACE

The Report published by the United Nations Fact Finding Mission on the Gaza Conflict, better known by the name of its head, as the "Goldstone Report" was a major breakthrough in three senses. In the first place the *Report* was the most systematic, detailed study of Israeli violations of international law in its wars against the Palestinian people. Secondly it caught the attention of the broadest sections of *world opinion* and ignited a firestorm of disapproval of Israel from almost all of the worlds' leaders.

On the negative side the publication of the Report and the vehement rejection by all of the mainstream American Jewish Organizations, revealed their utterly craven disregard for human rights on the one hand and their absolute power and control over Washington's policy toward the Middle East on the other. The US Congress voted by a margin of over ten to one to denounce the *Report* and instead support Israeli war crimes, as did the White House.

The texts and illustrations in this book provide graphic accounts and visual evidence of why Israel has provoked a worldwide 'Boycott, Divestment and Sanctions' campaign by human rights activists, trade unions and a multitude of other groups, including individuals in Israel and Jewish organizations in Europe and North America. The *Goldstone Report* is an in depth case study of Israel's war crimes in Gaza, including the blockade of such essential goods, as food and medicine, the systematic and deliberate targeting and destruction of civilian targets, including the murder of civilians in homes, schools and UN facilities; the use of weapons designed to inflect maximum pain and death to civilians (white phosphorous bombs); the gratuitous destruction of the foundations of civilian life including food production, water installations and sewage treatment facilities. Like their Nazi predecessors, the Israeli forces used Palestinian civilians as "human shields", rounded up thousands of civilians, including women and children who were forcibly detained, humiliated and tortured. The *Report* concludes that the actions of the Israeli Government could lead to a "competent court finding that crimes against humanity have been committed." The *Report* was approved by a vast majority in the United Nations General Assembly ...

While it was beyond the mandate of the UN to discuss other Israeli war crimes, the *Goldstone Report* did give fleeting reference to Israel's use of the same methods during its invasion of Lebanon in 2006.

What the *Goldstone Report* described with regard to Israel's savaging of Gaza has a long and ignoble history, which needs to be addressed, especially in light of what some liberal Zionists charge as "picking on" Israel. Most critics especially on the Left condemn *all* brutal acts of war and torture *whenever* they are committed, so this charge is a phony cover-up of Israel's *especially* brutal conduct from the founding of the state. .Israel holds 'world records' in the number of towns and villages ethnically cleansed (over 500 and counting); number of refugees deported (4 million and counting); number of homes demolished (60 thousand and continuing); and has imprisoned more civilians per capita than any other country (250,000 and growing). Israel is the country with the highest number of protective US Security Council vetoes (over 100) preventing the world body from condemning Israeli war crimes.

Here is the great political and moral challenge. How do we explain the US governments' sustained complicity with Israeli war crimes in the face of worldwide reprobation? How do we explain the utterly depraved conduct of the Obama White House and nearly 90% of the US Congress in denouncing the *Goldstone Report*? These and other related questions are addressed in the chapters discussing the political, economic and cultural power of the Presidents of the Major American Jewish organizations, including but not confined to AIPAC.

Even as I write these lines, April 25, 2010, the news from Washington is that Congress has passed a new war-sanctions act, by a 95% majority imposing a virtual blockade of Iran, authored by AIPAC and backed by all the major Americans Jewish organizations. With the exception of a handful of writers and anti-Zionist Jewish activists, the vast majority of the progressive leftist, Marxist, anti-war and Palestinian organizations and intellectuals, even those critical of the Congressional vote, in fear and cowardice, refuse to name the intellectual authors and political promoters of this vile act of Congress.

The *Goldstone Report* energized many, especially young Jews who were reticent to criticize Israel, to speak out against Israeli war crimes. A few cracks appeared in the Zionist monolith, as liberal lobbyists like J Street, condemned the Jewish State's excesses in Gaza. Hopeful signs, alas which were, in great part, dashed when it came time to raise a hue and cry about AIPAC and mainstream Jewish-organized backing for the war-sanctions act against Iran. The silence was deafening. The saying that the Jewish left's opposition to Israel war policies ends *when a war begins*, applies to the present war-sanctions bill.

The terrible power of the Zionist Power Configuration has run amok: the Jewish Congressional lobby, the liberals, progressives and neo-cons all together signed and promoted an act of Congress signed by over 330 Congress people rebuking Obama for publicly disagreeing with Netanyahu over the land grab in Arab Jerusalem. This book not only provides a detailed account and illustration of Israeli war crimes in Gaza but equally important it provides a comprehensive analysis of the reasons why more and more people are recognizing that the US Congress and White House are zionized occupied territory.

THE GOLDSTONE REPORT*

EXECUTIVE SUMMARY*

A. Introduction

1. On 3 April 2009, the President of the Human Rights Council established the United Nations Fact Finding Mission on the Gaza Conflict with the mandate "to investigate all violations of international human rights law and international humanitarian law that might have been committed at any time in the context of the military operations that were conducted in Gaza during the period from 27 December 2008 and 18 January 2009, whether before, during or after."

2. The President appointed Justice Richard Goldstone, former judge of the Constitutional Court of South Africa and former Prosecutor of the International Criminal Tribunals for the former Yugoslavia and Rwanda, to head the Mission. The other three appointed members were: Professor Christine Chinkin, Professor of International Law at the London School of Economics and Political Science, who was a member of the high-level fact-finding mission to Beit Hanoun (2008); Ms. Hina Jilani, Advocate of the Supreme Court of Pakistan and former Special Representative of the Secretary-General on the situation of human rights defenders, who was a member of the International Commission of Inquiry on Darfur (2004); and Colonel Desmond Travers, a former Officer in Ireland's Defence Forces and member of the Board of Directors of the Institute for International Criminal Investigations.

3. As is usual practice, the Office of the United Nations High Commissioner for Human Rights (OHCHR) established a secretariat to support the Mission.

* Officially titled HUMAN RIGHTS IN PALESTINE AND OTHER OCCUPIED ARAB TERRITORIES: Report of the United Nations Fact-Finding Mission on the Gaza Conflict, UN General Assembly Doc. A/HRC/12/48 25 September 2009, the *Goldstone Report* in its entirety can be found at found at < http://www2.ohchr.org/english/bodies/hrcouncil/docs/12session/A-HRC-12-48.pdf>

4. The Mission interpreted the mandate as requiring it to place the civilian population of the region at the centre of its concerns regarding the violations of international law.

5. The Mission convened for the first time in Geneva between 4 and 8 May 2009. Additionally, the Mission met in Geneva on 20 May, on 4 and 5 July, and between 1 and 4 August 2009. The Mission conducted three field visits: two to the Gaza Strip between 30 May and 6 June, and between 25 June and 1 July 2009; and one visit to Amman on 2 and 3 July 2009. Several staff of the Mission's secretariat were deployed in Gaza from 22 May to 4 July 2009 to conduct field investigations.

6. Notes verbales were sent to all Member States of the United Nations and United Nations organs and bodies on 7 May 2009. On 8 June 2009 the Mission issued a call for submissions inviting all interested persons and organizations to submit relevant information and documentation to assist in the implementation of its mandate.

7. Public hearings were held in Gaza on 28 and 29 June and in Geneva on 6 and 7 July 2009.

8. The Mission repeatedly sought to obtain the cooperation of the Government of Israel. After numerous attempts had failed, the Mission sought and obtained the assistance of the Government of Egypt to enable it to enter the Gaza Strip through the Rafah crossing.

9. The Mission has enjoyed the support and cooperation of the Palestinian Authority and of the Permanent Observer Mission of Palestine to the United Nations. Due to the lack of cooperation from the Israeli Government, the Mission was unable to meet members of the Palestinian Authority in the West Bank. The Mission did, however, meet officials of the Palestinian Authority, including a cabinet minister, in Amman. During its visits to the Gaza Strip, the Mission held meetings with senior members of the Gaza authorities and they extended their full cooperation and support to the Mission.

10. Subsequent to the public hearings in Geneva, the Mission was informed that a Palestinian participant, Mr. Muhammad Srour, had been detained by Israeli security forces when returning to the West Bank and became concerned that his detention may have been a consequence of his appearance before the Mission. The Mission is in contact with him and continues to monitor developments.

B. Methodology

11. To implement its mandate, the Mission determined that it was required to consider any actions by all parties that might have constituted violations of international human rights law or international humanitarian law. The mandate also required it to review related actions in the entire Occupied Palestinian Territory and Israel.

12. With regard to temporal scope, the Mission decided to focus primarily on events, actions or circumstances occurring since 19 June 2008, when a ceasefire was agreed between the Government of Israel and Hamas. The Mission has also taken into consideration matters occurring after the end of military operations that constitute continuing human rights and international humanitarian law violations related to or as a consequence of the military operations, up to 31 July 2009.

13. The Mission also analysed the historical context of the events that led to the military operations in Gaza between during the period from 27 December 2008 and 18 January 2009 and the links between these operations and overarching Israeli policies vis-à-vis the OccupiedPalestinian Territory.

14. The Mission considered that the reference in its mandate to violations committed "in the context" of the December–January military operations required it to include restrictions on human rights and fundamental freedoms relating to Israel's strategies and actions in the context of its military operations.

15. The normative framework for the Mission has been general international law, the Charter of the United Nations, international humanitarian law, international human rights law and international criminal law.

16. This report does not purport to be exhaustive in documenting the very high number of relevant incidents that occurred in the period covered by the Mission's mandate. Nevertheless, the Mission considers that the report is illustrative of the main patterns of violations. In Gaza, the Mission investigated 36 incidents.

17. The Mission based its work on an independent and impartial analysis of compliance by the parties with their obligations under international human rights and humanitarian law in the context of the recent conflict in Gaza, and on international investigative standards developed by the United Nations.

18. The Mission adopted an inclusive approach in gathering information and seeking views. Information-gathering methods included: (a) the review of reports from different sources; (b) interviews with victims, witnesses and other persons having relevant information); (c) site visits to specific locations in Gaza where incidents had occurred; (d) the analysis of video and photographic images, including satellite imagery; (e) the review of medical reports about injuries to victims; (f) the forensic analysis of weapons and ammunition remnants collected at incident sites; (g) meetings with a variety of interlocutors; (h) invitations to provide information relating to the Mission's investigation requirements; (i) the wide circulation of a public call for written submissions; (j) public hearings in Gaza and in Geneva;

19. The Mission conducted 188 individual interviews. It reviewed more than 300 reports, submissions and other documentation either researched of its own motion, received in reply to its call for submissions and notes verbales or provided during meetings or otherwise, amounting to more than 10,000 pages, over 30 videos and 1,200 photographs.

20. By refusing to cooperate with the Mission, the Government of Israel prevented it from meeting Israeli government officials, but also from travelling to Israel to meet with Israeli victims and to the West Bank to meet with Palestinian Authority representatives and Palestinian victims.

21. The Mission conducted field visits, including investigations of incident sites, in the Gaza Strip. This allowed the Mission to observe first-hand the situation on the ground, and speak to many witnesses and other relevant persons.

22. The purpose of the public hearings, which were broadcast live, was to enable victims, witnesses and experts from all sides to the conflict to speak directly to as many people as possible in the region as well as in the international community. The Mission gave priority to the participation of victims and people from the affected communities. The 38 public testimonies covered facts as well as legal and military matters. The Mission had initially intended to hold hearings in Gaza, Israel and the West Bank. However, denial of access to Israel and the West Bank resulted in the decision to hold hearings of participants from Israel and the West Bank in Geneva.

23. In establishing its findings, the Mission sought to rely primarily and whenever possible on information it gathered first-hand. Information produced by others, including reports, affidavits and media reports, was used primarily as corroboration.

24. The Mission's final conclusions on the reliability of the information received were made taking into consideration the Mission's assessment of the credibility and reliability of the witnesses it met, verifying sources and methodology used in reports and documents produced by others, cross-referencing the relevant material and information, and assessing whether, in all the circumstances, there was sufficient information of a credible and reliable nature for the Mission to make a finding in fact.

25. On this basis, the Mission has, to the best of its ability, determined what facts have been established. In many cases it has found that acts entailing individual criminal responsibility have been committed. In all of these cases the Mission has found that there is sufficient information to establish the objective elements of the crimes in question. In almost all of the cases the Mission has also been able to determine whether or not it appears that the acts in question were done deliberately or recklessly or in the knowledge that the consequence that resulted would result in the ordinary course of events. The Mission has thus referred in many cases to the relevant fault element (mens rea). The Mission fully appreciates the importance of the presumption of innocence: the findings in the report do not subvert the operation of that principle. The findings do not attempt to identify the individuals responsible for the commission of offences nor do they pretend to reach the standard of proof applicable in criminal trials.

26. In order to provide the parties concerned with an opportunity to submit additional relevant information and express their position and respond to allegations, the Mission also submitted comprehensive lists of questions to the Government of Israel, the Palestinian Authority and the Gaza authorities in advance of completing its analysis and findings. The Mission received replies from the Palestinian Authority and the Gaza authorities but not from Israel.

C. Facts investigated by the Mission, factual and legal findings

The Occupied Palestinian Territory: the Gaza Strip

1. The Blockade

27. The Mission focussed (Chapter V) on the process of economic and political isolation imposed by Israel on the Gaza Strip, generally referred to as a "blockade". The blockade comprises measures such as restrictions on the goods that can be imported into Gaza and the closure of border crossings for people, goods and services, sometimes for days, including cuts on the provision of fuel and electricity. Gaza's economy is further severely affected by the reduction of the fishing zone

open to the Palestinian fishermen and the establishment of a "buffer zone" along the border between Gaza and Israel which reduces the land available for agriculture and industrial activity. In addition to creating an emergency situation, the blockade significantly weakened the capacities of the population and of the health, water and other public sectors to react to the emergency created by the military operations.

28. The Mission holds the view that Israel continues to be duty-bound under the Fourth Geneva Convention and to the full extent of the means available to it to ensure the supply of foodstuff, medical and hospital items and others to meet the humanitarian needs of the population of the Gaza Strip without qualification.

2. Overview of Israel's military operations in the Gaza Strip and casualties

29. Israel deployed its navy, air force and army in the operation it codenamed "Operation Cast Lead". The military operations in the Gaza Strip included two main phases, the air phase and the air-land phase, and lasted from 27 December 2008 to 18 January 2009. The Israeli offensive began with a week-long air attack, from 27 December until 3 January 2009. The air force continued to play an important role in assisting and covering the ground forces from 3 January to18 January 2009. The army was responsible for the ground invasion, which began on 3 January 2009 when ground troops entered Gaza from the north and from the east. The available information indicates that the Golani, Givati and Paratrooper Brigades and five Armoured Corps Brigades were involved. The navy was used in part to shell the Gaza coast during the operations. Chapter VI also locates the incidents investigated by the Mission, described in Chapters VII to XV, in the context of the military operations.

30. Statistics about Palestinians who lost their life during the military operations vary. Based on extensive field research, non-governmental organizations place the overall number of persons killed between 1,387 and 1,417. The Gaza authorities report 1,444 fatal casualties. The Government of Israel provides a figure of 1,166. The data provided by non-governmental sources with regard to the percentage of civilians among those killed are generally consistent and raise very serious concerns with regard to the way Israel conducted the military operations in Gaza.

31. According to the Government of Israel, during the military operations there were 4 Israeli fatal casualties in southern Israel, of whom 3 were civilians and one soldier, killed by rockets and mortars attacks by Palestinian armed groups. In addition, 9 Israeli soldiers were killed

during the fighting inside the Gaza strip, 4 of whom as a result of friendly fire.

3. Attacks by Israeli forces on government buildings and persons of the Gaza authorities, including police

32. Israeli armed forces launched numerous attacks against buildings and persons of the Gaza authorities. As far as attacks on buildings are concerned, the Mission examined the Israeli strikes against the Palestinian Legislative Council and the Gaza main prison (Chapter VII). Both buildings were destroyed to an extent that puts them out of use. Statements by Israeli Government and armed forces representatives justified the attacks arguing that political and administrative institutions in Gaza are part of the "Hamas terrorist infrastructure". The Mission rejects this position. It finds that there is no evidence that the Legislative Council building and the Gaza main prison made an effective contribution to military action. On the information available to it, the Mission finds that the attacks on these buildings constituted deliberate attacks on civilian objects in violation of the rule of customary international humanitarian law whereby attacks must be strictly limited to military objectives. These facts further indicate the commission of the grave breach of extensive destruction of property, not justified by military necessity and carried out unlawfully and wantonly.

33. The Mission examined the attacks against six police facilities, four of them during the first minutes of the military operations on 27 December 2008, resulting in the death of 99 policemen and nine members of the public. The overall around 240 policemen killed by Israeli forces constitute more than one sixth of the Palestinian casualties. The circumstances of the attacks and the Government of Israel July 2009 report on the military operations clarify that the policemen were deliberately targeted and killed on the ground that the police as an institution, or a large part of the policemen individually, are in the Government of Israel's view part of the Palestinian military forces in Gaza.

34. To examine whether the attacks against the police were compatible with the principle of distinction between civilian and military objects and persons, the Mission analysed the institutional development of the Gaza police since Hamas took complete control of Gaza in July 2007 and merged the Gaza police with the "Executive Force" it had created after its election victory. The Mission finds that, while a great number of the Gaza policemen were recruited among Hamas supporters or members of Palestinian armed groups, the Gaza police were acivilian law-enforcement agency. The Mission also concludes that the policemen

killed on 27 December 2008 cannot be said to have been taking a direct part in hostilities and thus did not lose their civilian immunity from direct attack as civilians on this ground. The Mission accepts that there may be individual members of the Gaza police that were at the same time members of Palestinian armed groups and thus combatants. It concludes, however, that the attacks against the police facilities on the first day of the armed operations failed to strike an acceptable balance between the direct military advantage anticipated (i.e. the killing of those policemen who may have been members of Palestinian armed groups) and the loss of civilian life (i.e. the other policemen killed and members of the public who would inevitably have been present or in the vicinity), and therefore violated international humanitarian law.

4. Obligation to take feasible precautions to protect civilian population and objects by Palestinian armed groups in Gaza

35. The Mission examined whether and to what extent the Palestinian armed groups violated their obligation to exercise care and take feasible precautions to protect the civilian population in Gaza from the inherent dangers of the military operations (Chapter VIII). The Mission was faced with a certain reluctance by the persons it interviewed in Gaza to discuss the activities of the armed groups. On the basis of the information gathered, the Mission found that Palestinian armed groups were present in urban areas during the military operations and launched rockets from urban areas. It may be that the Palestinian combatants did not at all times adequately distinguish themselves from the civilian population. The Mission found no evidence, however, to suggest that Palestinian armed groups either directed civilians to areas where attacks were being launched or that they forced civilians to remain within the vicinity of the attacks.

36. Although the situations investigated by the Mission did not establish the use of mosques for military purposes or to shield military activities, it cannot exclude that this might have occurred in other cases. The Mission did not find any evidence to support the allegations that hospital facilities were used by the Gaza authorities or by Palestinian armed groups to shield military activities and that ambulances were used to transport combatants or for other military purposes. On the basis of its own investigations and the statements by UN officials, the Mission excludes that Palestinian armed groups engaged in combat activities from UN facilities that were used as shelters during the military operations. The Mission cannot, however, discount the possibility that Palestinian armed groups were active in the vicinity of such UN facilities and hospitals. While the conduct of hostilities in built-up areas does not, of itself, constitute a violation of international law, Palestinian armed groups,

where they launched attacks close to civilian or protected buildings, unnecessarily exposed the civilian population of Gaza to danger.

5. Obligation to take feasible precautions to protect civilian population and objects by Israel in Gaza

37. The Mission examined how Israeli forces discharged their obligation to take feasible precautions to protect the civilian population of Gaza, including particularly the obligation to give effective advance warning of attacks (Chapter IX). The Mission acknowledges the significant efforts made by Israel to issue warnings through telephone calls, leaflets and radio broadcasts and accepts that in some cases, particularly when the warnings were sufficiently specific, they encouraged residents to leave an area and get out of harm's way. However, the Mission also notes factors that significantly undermined the effectiveness of the warnings issued. These include the lack of specificity and thus credibility of many pre-recorded phone messages and leaflets. The credibility of instructions to move to city centres for safety was also diminished by the fact that the city centres themselves had been the subject of intense attacks during the air phase of the military operations. The Mission also examined the practice of dropping lighter explosives on roofs (so-called "roof knocking"). It concludes that this technique is not effective as a warning and constitutes a form of attack against the civilians inhabiting the building. Finally, the Mission stresses that the fact that a warning was issued does not relieve a commander and his subordinates of taking all other feasible measures to distinguish between civilians and combatants.

38. The Mission also examined the precautions taken by Israeli forces in the context of three specific attacks they launched. On 15 January 2009, the UNRWA field office compound in Gaza City came under shelling with high explosive and white phosphorous munitions. The Mission notes that the attack was extremely dangerous, as the compound offered shelter to between 600 and 700 civilians and contained a huge fuel depot. The Israeli forces continued the attack over several hours in spite of having been fully alerted to the risks they created. The Mission concludes that Israeli armed forces violated the customary international law requirement to take all feasible precautions in the choice of means and method of attack with a view to avoiding and in any event minimizing incidental loss of civilian life, injury to civilians and damage to civilian objects.

39. The Mission also finds that, on the same day, the Israeli forces directly and intentionally attacked the Al Quds Hospital in Gaza City and the adjacent ambulance depot with white phosphorous shells. The attack caused fires which took a whole day to extinguish and caused

panic among the sick and wounded who had to be evacuated. The Mission finds that no warning was given at any point of an imminent strike. On the basis of its investigation, the Mission rejects the allegation that fire was directed at Israeli forces from within the hospital.

40. The Mission also examined the intense artillery attacks, again including white phosphorous munitions, on Al Wafa hospital in eastern Gaza City, a facility for patients receiving long-term care and suffering from particularly serious injuries. On the basis of the information gathered, the Mission found a violation of the prohibition of attacks on civilian hospitals in the cases of both hospitals. The Mission also highlights that the warnings given by leaflets and pre-recorded phone messages in the case of Al Wafa hospital demonstrate the complete ineffectiveness of certain kinds of routine and generic warnings.

6. Indiscriminate attacks by Israeli forces resulting in the loss of life and injury to civilians

41. The Mission examined the mortar shelling of al-Fakhura junction in Jabalya next to a UNRWA school which at the time was used as a shelter housing more than 1,300 people (Chapter X). The Israeli forces launched at least four mortar shells. One landed in the courtyard of a family home, killing eleven people assembled there. Three other shells landed on al-Fakhura Street, killing at least a further 24 people and injuring as many as 40. The Mission examines in detail statements by Israeli Government representatives alleging that the attack was launched in response to a mortar attack from an armed Palestinian group. While the Mission does not exclude that this may have been the case, it considers the credibility of Israel's position damaged by the series of inconsistencies, contradictions and factual inaccuracies in the statements justifying the attack.

42. In drawing its legal conclusions on the attack against al-Fakhura junction, the Mission recognizes that for all armies proportionality decisions, weighing the military advantage to be gained against the risk of killing civilians, will present very genuine dilemmas in certain cases. The Mission does not consider this to be such a case. The firing of at least four mortar shells to attempt to kill a small number of specified individuals in a setting where large numbers of civilians were going about their daily business and 1,368 people were sheltering nearby cannot meet the test of what a reasonable commander would have determined to be an acceptable loss of civilian life for the military advantage sought. The Mission considers thus the attack to have been indiscriminate in violation of international law, and to have violated the right to life of the Palestinian civilians killed in these incidents.

7. Deliberate attacks against the civilian population

43. The Mission investigated eleven incidents in which Israeli forces launched direct attacks against civilians with lethal outcome (Chapter XI). The cases examined in this part of the report are, with one exception, all cases in which the facts indicate no justifiable military objective pursued by the attack. The first two incidents are attacks against houses in the Samouni neighbourhood south of Gaza City, including the shelling of a house in which Palestinian civilians had been forced to assemble by the Israeli forces. The following group of seven incidents concern the shooting of civilians while they were trying to leave their homes to walk to a safer place, waving white flags and, in some of the cases, following an injunction from the Israeli forces to do so. The facts gathered by the Mission indicate that all the attacks occurred under circumstances in which the Israeli forces were in control of the area and had previously entered into contact with or at least observed the persons they subsequently attacked, so that they must have been aware of their civilian status. In the majority of these incidents, the consequences of the Israeli attacks against civilians were aggravated by their subsequent refusal to allow the evacuation of the wounded or to permit access to ambulances.

44. These incidents indicate that the instructions given to the Israeli forces moving into Gaza provided for a low threshold for the use of lethal fire against the civilian population. The Mission found strong corroboration of this trend emerging from its fact-finding in the testimonies of Israeli soldiers collected in two publications it reviewed.

45. The Mission further examined an incident in which a mosque was targeted with a missile during the early evening prayer, resulting in the death of fifteen, and an attack with flechette munitions on a crowd of family and neighbours at a condolence tent, killing five. The Mission finds that both attacks constitute intentional attacks against the civilian population and civilian objects.

46. From the facts ascertained in all the above cases, the Mission finds that the conduct of the Israeli armed forces constitute grave breaches of the Fourth Geneva Convention in respect of wilful killings and wilfully causing great suffering to protected persons and as such give rise to individual criminal responsibility. It also finds that the direct targeting and arbitrary killing of Palestinian civilians is a violation of the right to life.

47. The last incident concerns the launch of a bomb on a house resulting in the killing of 22 family members. Israel's position in this case is that there was an "operational error" and that the intended target was a

neighbouring house storing weapons. On the basis of its investigation, the Mission expresses significant doubts about the Israeli authorities' account of the incident. The Mission concludes that, if indeed a mistake was made, there could not be said to be a case of wilful killing. State responsibility of Israel for an internationally wrongful act, however, would remain.

8. The use of certain weapons

48. Based on its investigation of incidents involving the use of certain weapons such as white phosphorous and flechette missiles, the Mission, while accepting that white phosphorous is not at this stage proscribed under international law, finds that the Israeli armed forces were systematically reckless in determining its use in built-up areas. Moreover, doctors who treated patients with white phosphorous wounds spoke about the severity and sometimes untreatable nature of the burns caused by the substance. The Mission believes that serious consideration should be given to banning the use of white phosphorous in built-up areas. As to flechettes, the Mission notes that they are an area weapon incapable of discriminating between objectives after detonation. They are, therefore, particularly unsuitable for use in urban settings where there is reason to believe civilians may be present.

49. While the Mission is not in a position to state with certainty that so-called dense inert metal explosive (DIME) munitions were used by the Israeli armed forces, it did receive reports from Palestinian and foreign doctors who operated in Gaza during the military operations of a high percentage of patients with injuries compatible with their impact. DIME weapons and weapons armed with heavy metal are not prohibited under international law as it currently stands, but do raise specific health concerns. Finally, the Mission received allegations that depleted and nondepleted uranium were used by Israeli forces in Gaza. These allegations were not further investigated by the Mission.

9. Attacks on the foundations of civilian life in Gaza: destruction of industrial infrastructure, food production, water installations, sewage treatment and housing

50. The Mission investigated several incidents involving the destruction of industrial infrastructure, food production, water installations, sewage treatment and housing (Chapter XIII). Already at the beginning of the military operations, the Al Bader flour mill was the only flour mill in the Gaza Strip still operating. The flour mill was hit by a series of air strikes on 9 January 2009 after several false warnings had been issued on previous days. The Mission finds that its destruction had no military

justification. The nature of the strikes, in particular the precise targeting of crucial machinery, suggests that the intention was to disable the factory in terms of its productive capacity. From the facts it ascertained, the Mission finds that there has been a violation of the grave breaches provisions of the Fourth Geneva Convention. Unlawful and wanton destruction which is not justified by military necessity amounts to a war crime. The Mission also finds that the destruction of the mill was carried out for the purposes of denying sustenance to the civilian population, which is a violation of customary international law and may constitute a war crime. The strike on the flour mill further constitutes a violation of human rights provisions regarding the right to adequate food and means of subsistence.

51. The chicken farms of Mr. Sameh Sawafeary in the Zeitoun neighbourhood south of Gaza City reportedly supplied over 10 per cent of the Gaza egg market. Armoured bulldozers of the Israeli forces systematically flattened the chicken coops, killing all 31,000 chickens inside, and destroyed the plant and material necessary for the business. The Mission concludes that this was a deliberate act of wanton destruction not justified by any military necessity and draws the same legal conclusions as in the case of the destruction of the flour mill.

52. Israeli forces also carried out a strike against a wall of one of the raw sewage lagoons of the Gaza Waste Water Treatment Plant, which caused the outflow of more than 200,000 cubic metres of raw sewage into neighbouring farmland. The circumstances of the strike on the lagoon suggest that it was deliberate and premeditated. The Namar Wells complex in Jabalya consisted of two water wells, pumping machines, a generator, fuel storage, a reservoir chlorination unit, buildings and related equipment. All were destroyed by multiple air strikes on the first day of the Israeli aerial attack. The Mission considers it unlikely that a target the size of the Namar Wells could have been hit by multiple strikes in error. It found no grounds to suggest that there was any military advantage to be had by hitting the wells and noted that there was no suggestion that Palestinian armed groups had used the wells for any purpose. Considering that the right to drinking water is part of the right to adequate food, the Mission makes the same legal findings as in the case of the Al Bader flour mill.

53. During its visits to the Gaza Strip, the Mission witnessed the extent of the destruction of residential housing caused by air strikes, mortar and artillery shelling, missile strikes, the operation of bulldozers and demolition charges. In some cases, residential neighbourhoods were subjected to air-launched bombing and to intensive shelling apparently in the context of the advance of Israeli ground forces. In other cases,

the facts gathered by the Mission strongly suggest that the destruction of housing was carried out in the absence of any link to combat engagements with Palestinian armed groups or any other effective contribution to military action.

Combining the results of its own fact finding on the ground with UNOSAT imagery and the published testimonies of Israeli soldiers, the Mission concludes that, in addition to the extensive destruction of housing for so-called "operational necessity" during their advance, the Israeli forces engaged in another wave of systematic destruction of civilian buildings during the last three days of their presence in Gaza, aware of the imminence of withdrawal. The conduct of the Israeli forces in this respect violated the principle of distinction between civilian and military objects and amounted to the grave breach of "extensive destruction ... of property, not justified by military necessity and carried out unlawfully and wantonly". Israeli forces further violated the right to adequate housing of the families concerned.

54. The attacks on industrial facilities, food production and water infrastructure investigated by the Mission are part of a broader pattern of destruction, which includes the destruction of the only cement packaging plant in Gaza (the Atta Abu Jubbah plant), the Abu Eida factories for ready-mix concrete, further chicken farms and the Al Wadia Group's foods and drinks factories. The facts ascertained by the Mission indicate that there was a deliberate and systematic policy on the part of the Israeli armed forces to target industrial sites and water installations.

10. The use of Palestinian civilians as human shields

55. The Mission investigated four incidents in which Israeli forces coerced Palestinian civilian men at gun point to take part in house searches during the military operations (Chapter XIV). The Palestinian men were blindfolded and handcuffed as they were forced to enter houses ahead of the Israeli soldiers. In one of the incidents, Israeli forces repeatedly forced a man to enter a house in which Palestinian combatants were hiding. Published testimonies of Israeli soldiers who took part in the military operations confirm the continued use of this practice, in spite of clear orders from Israel's High Court to the armed forces to put an end to it and repeated public assurances from the armed forces that the practice had been discontinued. The Mission concludes that this practice amounts to the use of Palestinian civilians as human shields and is therefore prohibited by international humanitarian law. It puts the right to life of the civilians at risk in an arbitrary and unlawful manner and constitutes cruel and inhuman treatment. The use of human shields also is a war crime. The Palestinian men used as human shields

were questioned under threat of death or injury to extract information about Hamas, Palestinian combatants and tunnels. This constitutes a further violation of international humanitarian law.

11. Deprivation of liberty: Gazans detained during the Israeli operation of 27 December 2008 to 18 January 2009

56. During the military operations Israeli armed forces rounded up large numbers of civilians and detained them in houses and open spaces in Gaza and, in the case of many Palestinian men, also took them to detention facilities in Israel. In the cases investigated by the Mission, the facts gathered indicate that none of the civilians were armed or posed any apparent threat to the Israeli soldiers. Chapter XV of the report is based on the Mission's interviews with Palestinian men who were detained, as well as on the Mission's review of other relevant material, including interviews with relatives and statements from other victims submitted to the Mission.

57. From the facts gathered, the Mission finds that there were numerous violations of international humanitarian law and human rights law committed in the context of these detentions. Civilians, including women and children, were detained in degrading conditions, deprived of food, water and access to sanitary facilities, and exposed to the elements in January without any shelter. The men were handcuffed, blindfolded and repeatedly made to strip,sometimes naked, at different stages of their detention.

58. In the Al Atatra area in north-western Gaza Israeli troops had dug out sand pits in which Palestinian men, women and children were detained. Israeli tanks and artillery positions were located inside the sand pits and around them and fired from next to the detainees.

59. The Palestinian men who were taken to detention facilities in Israel were subjected to degrading conditions of detention, harsh interrogation, beatings and other physical and mental abuse. Some of them were charged with being unlawful combatants. Those interviewed by the Mission were released after the proceedings against them had apparently been discontinued.

60. In addition to arbitrary deprivation of liberty and violation of due process rights, the cases of the detained Palestinian civilians highlight a common thread of the interaction between Israeli soldiers and Palestinian civilians which emerged clearly also in many cases discussed in other parts of the Report: continuous and systematic abuse, outrages on personal dignity, humiliating and degrading treatment

contrary to fundamental principles of international humanitarian law and human rights law. The Mission concludes that the treatment of these civilians constitutes the infliction of a collective penalty on those persons and amounts to measures of intimidation and terror. Such acts are grave breaches of the Geneva Conventions and constitute a war crime.

12. Objectives and strategy of Israel's military operations in Gaza
61. The Mission reviewed available information on the planning of the Israeli military operations in Gaza, on the advanced military technology available to the Israeli forces and on their training in international humanitarian law (Chapter XVI). According to official Government information, the Israeli armed forces have an elaborate legal advice and training system in place, which seeks to ensure knowledge of the relevant legal obligations and support to commanders for compliance in the field. The Israeli armed forces possess very advanced hardware and are also a market leader in the production of some of the most advanced pieces of military technology available, including UAVs. They have a very significant capacity for precision strikes by a variety of methods, including aerial and ground launches. Taking into account the ability to plan, the means to execute plans with the most developed technology available, and statements by the Israeli military that almost no errors occurred, the Mission finds that the incidents and patterns of events considered in the report are the result of deliberate planning and policy decisions.

62. The tactics used by Israeli military armed forces in the Gaza offensive are consistent with previous practices, most recently during the Lebanon war in 2006. A concept known as the Dahiya doctrine emerged then, involving the application of disproportionate force and the causing of great damage and destruction to civilian property and infrastructure, and suffering to civilian populations. The Mission concludes from a review of the facts on the ground that it witnessed for itself that what was prescribed as the best strategy appears to have been precisely what was put into practice.

63. In the framing of Israeli military objectives with regard to the Gaza operations, the concept of Hamas' "supporting infrastructure" is particularly worrying as it appears to transform civilians and civilian objects into legitimate targets. Statements by Israeli political and military leaders prior to and during the military operations in Gaza indicate that the Israeli military conception of what was necessary in a war with Hamas viewed disproportionate destruction and creating the maximum disruption in the lives of many people as a legitimate means to achieve not only military but also political goals.

64. Statements by Israeli leaders to the effect that the destruction of civilian objects would be justified as a response to rocket attacks ("destroy 100 homes for every rocket fired"), indicate the possibility of resort to reprisals. The Mission is of the view that reprisals against civilians in armed hostilities are contrary to international humanitarian law.

13. The impact of the military operations and of the blockade on the Gaza population and their human rights

65. The Mission examined the combined impact of the military operations and of the blockade on the Gaza population and its enjoyment of human rights. The economy, employment opportunities and family livelihoods were already severely affected by the blockade when the Israeli offensive began. Insufficient supply of fuel for electricity generation had a negative impact on industrial activity, on the operation of hospitals, on water supply to households and on sewage treatment. Import restrictions and the ban on all exports from Gaza affected the industrial sector and agricultural production. Unemployment levels and the percentage of the population living in poverty and deep poverty were rising.

66. In this precarious situation, the military operations destroyed a substantial part of the economic infrastructure. As a large part of the factories were targeted and destroyed or damaged, poverty, unemployment and food insecurity further increased dramatically. The agricultural sector similarly suffered due to the destruction of agricultural land, water wells and fishing boats during the military operations. The continuation of the blockade impedes the reconstruction of the economic infrastructure destroyed.

67. As a result of the razing of farmland and destruction of greenhouses, food insecurity is expected to further worsen in spite of the increased quantities of food items allowed into Gaza since the beginning of the military operations. Dependence on food assistance increases. Levels of stunting and thinness in children and of anaemia prevalence in children and pregnant women were worrying already before the military operations. The hardship caused by the extensive destruction of shelter (UNDP reported 3,354 houses completely destroyed and 11,112 partially damaged) and resulting displacement particularly affects children and women. In the water and sanitation sector, the destruction of infrastructure (such as the destruction of the Namar wells and the attack against the water treatment plant described in Chapter XIII), aggravated the preexisting situation. Already before the military operations, 80 percent of the water supplied in Gaza did not meet the

WHO's standards for drinking water. The discharge of untreated or partially treated waste water into the sea is a further health hazard worsened by the military operations.

68. The military operations and resulting casualties subjected the beleaguered Gaza health sector to additional strain. Hospitals and ambulances were targeted by Israeli attacks. Patients with chronic health conditions could not be given priority in hospitals faced with the influx of patients with life-threatening injuries. Patients with hostilities-related injuries had often to be discharged as early as possible to free beds. The long term health impact of these early discharges, as well as of weapons containing substances such as tungsten and white phosphorous, remains a source of concern. While the exact number of people who will suffer permanent disabilities is still unknown, the Mission understands that many persons who sustained traumatic injuries during the conflict still face the risk of permanent disability due to complications and inadequate follow-up and physical rehabilitation.
69. The number of persons suffering from mental health problems is also bound to increase. The Mission investigated a number of incidents in which adults and children witnessed the killing of their loved ones. Doctors of the Gaza Community Mental Health Programme gave information to the Mission on psychosomatic disorders, on a widespread state of alienation in the population, and on "numbness" as a result of severe loss. They told the Mission that these conditions were likely to in turn increase the readiness to embrace violence and extremism. They also told the Mission that 20 percent of children in the Gaza Strip suffer Post Traumatic Stress Disorders.

70. Children's learning difficulties of psychological origin are compounded by the impact of the blockade and the military operations on the education infrastructure. 280 schools and kindergartens were destroyed in a situation in which already restrictions on the importation of construction materials meant that many school buildings were in serious need of repair.

71. The Mission's attention was also drawn to the particular manner in which women were affected by the military operations. The cases of women interviewed by the Mission in Gaza dramatically illustrate the suffering resulting from the feeling of inability to provide children with the care and security they need. Women's responsibility for the household and the children often forces them to conceal their own sufferings, resulting in their issues remaining unaddressed. The number of women who are sole breadwinners increased, but their employment opportunities remain significantly inferior to men's. The military operations and increased poverty add to the potential for conflicts in

the family and among widowed women and their inlaws.

72. The Mission acknowledges that the supply of humanitarian goods, particularly foodstuffs, allowed into Gaza by Israel temporarily increased during the military operations. The level of goods allowed into Gaza before the military operations, however, was insufficient to meet the needs of the population even before hostilities started, and has again decreased after the end of the military operations. From the facts ascertained by it, the Mission believes that Israel has violated its obligation to allow free passage of all consignments of medical and hospital objects, food and clothing (article 23 of the Fourth Geneva Convention). The Mission also finds that Israel violated specific obligations it has as Occupying Power spelled out in the Fourth Geneva Convention, such as the duty to maintain medical and hospital establishments and services and to agree to relief schemes if the occupied territory is not well supplied.

73. The Mission also concludes that in the destruction by Israeli armed forces of private residential houses, water wells, water tanks, agricultural land and greenhouses there was a specific purpose of denying them for their sustenance to the population of the Gaza Strip. The Mission finds that Israel violated its duty to respect the right of the Gaza population to an adequate standard of living, including access to adequate food, water and housing. The Mission moreover finds violations of specific human rights provisions protecting the rights of children, particularly those who are victims of armed conflict, women and the disabled.

74. The conditions of life in Gaza, resulting from deliberate actions of the Israeli forces and the declared policies of the Government of Israel – as they were presented by its authorized and legitimate representatives - with regard to the Gaza Strip before, during and after the military operation, cumulatively indicate the intention to inflict collective punishment on the people of the Gaza Strip in violation of international humanitarian law.

75. Finally, the Mission considered whether the series of acts that deprive Palestinians in the Gaza Strip of their means of sustenance, employment, housing and water, that deny their freedom of movement and their right to leave and enter their own country, that limit their access a court of law and an effective remedy, could amount to persecution, a crime against humanity. From the facts available to it, the Mission is of the view that some of the actions of the Government of Israel might justify a competent court finding that crimes against humanity have been committed.

14. The continuing detention of Israeli soldier Gilad Shalit

76. The Mission notes the continued detention of Gilad Shalit, a member of the Israeli armed forces, captured in 2006 by a Palestinian armed group. In reaction to his capture, the Israeli Government ordered a number of attacks against infrastructure in the Gaza Strip and Palestinian Authority offices as well as the arrest of eight Palestinian Government ministers and 26 members of the Palestinian Legislative Council. The Mission heard testimonies indicating that during the military operations of December 2008 – January 2009, Israeli soldiers questioned captured Palestinians about the whereabouts of Gilad Shalit. Gilad Shalit's father, Noam Shalit, appeared before the Mission at the public hearing held in Geneva on 6 July 2009.

77. The Mission is of the opinion that, as a soldier who belongs to the Israeli armed forces andwho was captured during an enemy incursion into Israel, Gilad Shalit meets the requirements for prisoner-of-war status under the Third Geneva Convention. As such, he should be protected, treated humanely and be allowed external communication as appropriate according to that Convention. The ICRC should be allowed to visit him without delay. Information about his condition should also be provided promptly to his family.

78. The Mission is concerned by declarations made by various Israeli officials, who have indicated the intention of maintaining the blockade of the Gaza Strip until the release of Gilad Shalit. The Mission is of the opinion that this would constitute collective punishment of the civilian population of the Gaza Strip.

15. Internal violence and targeting of Fateh affiliates by security services under the control of the Gaza authorities

79. The Mission obtained information about violence against political opponents by the security services that report to the Gaza authorities. These included killing of a number of Gaza residents between the beginning of the Israeli military operations and 27 February. Among these were some detainees who had been at al-Saraya detention facility on 28 December, and who had fled following the Israeli aerial attack. Not all those killed after escaping detention were Fatah affiliates, detained for political reasons, or charged with collaborating with the enemy. Some of the escapees had been convicted of serious crimes, such as drug-dealing or murder, and had been sentenced to death. The Mission was informed that the movement of many Fatah members was restricted during Israel's military operations in Gaza and that many were put under house arrest. According to the Gaza authorities, arrests

were made only after the end of the Israeli military operations and only in relation to criminal acts and to restore public order.

80. The Mission gathered first-hand information on five cases of Fatah affiliates detained, killed or subject to physical abuse by members of security forces or armed groups in Gaza. In most cases those abducted from their homes or otherwise detained were reportedly not accused of offences related to specific incidents, but rather targeted because of their political affiliation. When charges were laid, these were always linked to suspected political activities. The testimonies of witnesses and the reports provided by international and domestic human rights organizations bear striking similarities and indicate that these attacks were not randomly executed, but constituted part of a pattern of organized violence directed mainly against Fatah affiliates and supporters. The Mission finds that such actions constitute serious violations of human rights and are not consistent with either the Universal Declaration of Human Rights or the Palestinian Basic Law.

The Occupied Palestinian Territory: the West Bank, including East Jerusalem

81. The Mission considered developments in Gaza and the West Bank as closely interrelated, and analysed both to reach an informed understanding of and to report on issues within the Mission's mandate.

82. A consequence of Israel's non-cooperation with the Mission was that the Mission was unable to visit the West Bank to investigate alleged violations of international law there. However, the Mission has received many oral and written reports and other relevant materials from Palestinian, Israeli and international human rights organizations and institutions. In addition, the Mission has met with representatives of human rights organizations, members of the Palestinian legislature and community leaders. It heard experts, witnesses and victims in the public hearings, interviewed affected individuals and witnesses and reviewed video and photographic material.

16. Treatment of Palestinians by Israeli security forces in the West Bank, including use of excessive or lethal force during demonstrations

83. Various witnesses and experts informed the Mission of a sharp increase in the use of force by the Israeli security forces against Palestinians in the West Bank from the commencement of the Israeli operations in Gaza (Chapter XIX). A number of protestors were killed by Israeli forces during Palestinian demonstrations, including in support

of the Gaza population under attack, following the beginning of the operations, and scores were injured. The level of violence employed in the West Bank during the time of the operation in Gaza, was sustained also after the end of the operation.

84. Of particular concern to the Mission were allegations of the use of unnecessary, lethal force by Israeli security forces, the use of live ammunitions, and the provision in the Israeli armed forces "open fire regulations" of different rules to deal with disturbances where only Palestinians are present, as compared to disturbances where Israelis are present. This raises serious concern with regard to discriminatory policies vis-à-vis Palestinians. Eye-witnesses also reported to the Mission the use of sniper fire in the context of crowd control. Witnesses spoke of the markedly different atmosphere they encountered in the confrontation with the soldiers and border police during demonstrations in which all checks and balances had been removed. Several witnesses told the Mission that during the operation in Gaza, the sense in the West Bank was one of a "free for all", where anything was permitted.

85. Little if any action is taken by Israeli authorities to investigate, prosecute and punish violence against Palestinians by settlers and members of security forces, including killings, resulting in a situation of impunity. The Mission concludes that Israel has failed to fulfill its obligations to protect the Palestinians from violence by private individuals under both international human rights law and international humanitarian law.

17. Detention of Palestinians in Israeli prisons

86. It is estimated that since the beginning of the occupation, approximately 700,000 Palestinian men, women and children have been detained by Israel. According to estimates, as at 1st June 2009, there were approximately 8,100 Palestinian 'political prisoners' in detention in Israel, including 60 women and 390 children. Most of these detainees are charged or convicted by the Israeli Military Court System that operates for Palestinians in the West Bank and under which due process rights for Palestinians are severely limited. Many are held in administrative detention, and some under the Israeli "Unlawful Combatants Law".

87. The Mission focussed on a number of issues in relation to Palestinian detainees that in its view are linked to the December-January Israeli military operations in Gaza or their context.

88. Legal measures since Israel's disengagement from Gaza in 2005 have resulted in differential treatment for Gazan detainees. A 2006

law altered due process guarantees, and is applied only to Palestinian suspects, the overwhelming majority of whom are from Gaza according to Israeli government sources. The ICRC Family Visits Programme in the Gaza Strip was suspended in 2007, barring all means of communication between Gazan prisoners and the outside world.

89. During the Israeli military operations in Gaza, the number of children detained by Israel increased compared to the same period in 2008. Many children were reportedly arrested on the street and/or during demonstrations in the West Bank during the Gaza operations. Numbers of child detainees continued to be high in the months following the end of the operations, accompanied by reports of abuses by Israeli security forces.

90. A feature of Israel's detention practice vis-à-vis the Palestinians since 2005 has been the arrest of persons affiliated with Hamas. A few months before the Palestinian Legislative Council (PLC) elections in 2005, Israel arrested numerous persons who had been involved in municipal or PLC elections. Following the capture by Palestinian armed groups of Israeli soldier Gilad Shalit in June 2006, the Israeli army arrested some 65 members of the PLC, Mayors and Ministers, mostly Hamas members. All were held at least two years, generally in inadequate conditions. Further arrests of Hamas leaders were conducted during the Gaza military operations. The detention of the PLC members has meant that the PLC has been unable to function and exercise its legislative and oversight function over the Palestinian executive.

91. The Mission finds that these practices have resulted in violations of international human rights and humanitarian law, including the prohibition of arbitrary detention, the right to equal protection under the law and not to be discriminated based on political beliefs and the special protections to which children are entitled. The Mission also finds that the detention of PLC members may amount to collective punishment contrary to international humanitarian law.

18. Restrictions on freedom of movement in the West Bank

92. In the West Bank, Israel has long imposed a system of movement restrictions. Movement is restricted by a combination of physical obstacles such as roadblocks, checkpoints and the Wall, but also through administrative measures such as identity cards, permits, assigned residence, laws on family reunification, and policies on the right to enter from abroad and the right of return for refugees. Palestinians are denied access to areas expropriated for the building of the Wall and its infrastructure, for use by settlements, buffer zones, military bases and military training zones, and the roads built to connect these places.

Many of these roads are "Israeli only" and forbidden for Palestinian use. Tens of thousands of Palestinians today are subject to a "travel ban" imposed by Israel, preventing them from travelling abroad. A number of witnesses and experts invited by the Mission to meet in Amman and participate in the hearings in Geneva could not meet with the Mission due to this travel ban.

93. The Mission has received reports that, during the Israeli offensive in Gaza, movement restrictions in the West Bank were tightened. Israel imposed a "closure" on the West Bank for several days. Additionally there were a greater number of checkpoints in the West Bank, including in East Jerusalem, for the duration of the operation. Most of these were so-called "flying" checkpoints. In January 2009, several areas of the West Bank between the Wall and the Green line were declared "closed military areas".

94. During and following the operations in Gaza, Israel deepened its hold on the West Bank through an increased level of expropriation, an increased number of house demolitions, demolition orders and of permits granted for homes built in settlements, and increased exploitation of the natural resources in the West Bank. Following the operations in Gaza, Israel has amended the regulations which determine the ability of persons with "Gaza ID" to move to the West Bank, and vice versa, further entrenching the separation between the people of the West Bank and Gaza.

95. Israel's Ministry of Housing and Planning is planning a further 73,000 settlement homes to be built in the West Bank. The building of 15,000 of these homes has already been approved, and, if all the plans are realized, the number of settlers in the occupied Palestinian territory will be doubled.

96. The Mission believes that the movement and access restrictions to which West Bank Palestinians are subject are disproportionate to any military objective served, in general, and more so in relation to the increased restrictions during and to some extent after the military operation in Gaza. In addition, the Mission is concerned about the steps taken recently to formalise the separation between Gaza and the West Bank, and as such between two parts of the OPT.

19. Internal violence and targeting of Hamas supporters by the Palestinian Authority, restrictions on freedom of expression and assembly

97. The Mission has received allegations of violations relevant to its

mandate committed by the Palestinian Authority in the period under inquiry. These include violations related to the treatment of (suspected) Hamas affiliates by the security services, including unlawful arrest and detention. Several Palestinian human rights organizations have reported that practices used by the Palestinian Authority security forces in the West Bank amount to torture and cruel, inhuman and degrading treatment and punishment. There have been a number of cases of death in detention where it is suspected that torture and other ill treatment may have contributed to, or caused, the death of the detainee. Complaints of such practices have not been investigated.

98. Allegations were also received in relation to the use of excessive force and suppression of demonstrations by Palestinian security services—particularly those in support of the population of Gaza during the Israeli military operations. On these occasions Palestinian Authority security services have allegedly arrested many individuals and prevented the media from covering the events. The Mission also received allegations of harassment by Palestinian security services of journalists who expressed critical views.

99. The disabling of the Palestinian Legislative Council following the arrest and detention by Israel of several of its members has effectively curtailed parliamentary oversight over the PA executive. The executive has passed a number of decrees and regulations to enable its day to day functioning.

100. Other allegations include the arbitrary closure of Hamas and other Islamic groups affiliated charities and associations or the revocation and non-renewal of their licenses, the forcible replacement of board members of Islamic schools and other institutions and the dismissal of Hamas affiliated teachers.

101. The Palestinian Authority continues to discharge a large number of civil and military service employees, or suspend their salaries, under the pretext of "non-adherence to the legitimate authority" or "non-obtainment of security approval" on their appointments, which has become a pre-requirement for enrolment in public service". In effect, this measure means the exclusion of Hamas supporters or affiliates from public sector appointment.

102. The Mission is of the view that the reported measures are inconsistent with the Palestinian Authority's obligations deriving from the Universal Declaration on Human Rights (UDHR) and the Palestinian Basic Law.

Israel

20. Impact on civilians of rocket and mortar attacks by Palestinian armed groups on southern Israel

103. Palestinian armed groups have launched about 8000 rockets and mortars into southern Israel since 2001 (Chapter XIII). While communities such as Sderot and Kibbutz Nir-Am have been within the range of rocket and mortar fire since the beginning, the range of rocket fire increased to nearly 40 kilometres from the Gaza border, encompassing towns as far north as Ashdod, during the Israeli military operations in Gaza.

104. Since 18 June 2008, rockets fired by Palestinian armed groups in Gaza have killed 3 civilians inside Israel and 2 civilians in Gaza when a rocket landed short of the border on 26 December 2008. Reportedly, over 1000 civilians inside Israel were physically injured as a result of rocket and mortar attacks, 918 of which were injured during the time of the Israeli military operations in Gaza.

105. The Mission has taken particular note of the high level of psychological trauma suffered by the civilian population inside Israel. Data gathered by an Israeli organization in October 2007 found that 28.4% of adults and 72-94% of children in Sderot suffered from Post-Traumatic Stress Disorder. 1596 people were reportedly treated for stress-related injuries during the military operations in Gaza while over 500 people were treated following the end of the operations.

106. Rocke and mortars have damaged houses, schools and cars in southern Israel. On 5 March 2009, a rocket struck a synagogue in Netivot. The rocket and mortar fire has adversely impacted on the right to education of children and adults living in southern Israel. This is a result of school closures and interruptions to classes by alerts and moving to shelters and also the diminished ability to learn that is witnessed in individual experiencing symptoms of psychological trauma.

107. The rocket and mortar fire has also adversely impacted on the economic and social life of the affected communities. For communities such as Ashdod, Yavne, Beer Sheba, which experienced rocket strikes for the first time during the Israeli military operations in Gaza, there was a brief interruption to their economy and cultural brought about by the temporary displacement of some of their residents. For towns closer to the Gaza border that have been under rocket and mortar fire since 2001, the recent escalation has added to the exodus of residents from these areas.

108. The Mission has determined that the rockets and, to a lesser extent, mortars, fired by the Palestinian armed groups are incapable of being directed towards specific military objectives and were fired into areas where civilian populations are based. The Mission has further determined that these attacks constitute *indiscriminate* attacks upon the civilian population of southern Israel and that where there is no intended military target and the rockets and mortars are launched into a civilian population, they constitute a *deliberate* attack against a civilian population. These acts would constitute war crimes and may amount to crimes against humanity. Given the seeming inability of the Palestinian armed groups to direct the rockets and mortars towards specific targets and given the fact that the attacks have caused very little damage to Israeli military assets, the Mission finds that there is significant evidence to suggest that one of the primary purposes of the rocket and mortar attacks is to spread terror amongst the Israeli civilian population, a violation of international law.

109. Noting that some of the Palestinian armed groups, along them Hamas, have publicly expressed an intention to target civilians as reprisals for the fatalities of civilians in Gaza as a result of Israeli military operations, the Mission is of the view that reprisals against civilians in armed hostilities are contrary to international humanitarian law.

110. The Mission notes that the relatively few casualties sustained by civilians inside Israel is due in large part to the precautions put into place by Israel. This includes an early warning system, the provision of public shelters and fortifications of schools and other public buildings at great financial cost – a projected USD 460 million between 2005 and 2011- to the Government of Israel. The Mission is greatly concerned, however, about the lack of an early warning system and a lack of public shelters and fortifications available to the Palestinian Israeli communities living unrecognised and in some of the recognised villages that are within the range of rocket and mortars being fired by Palestinian armed groups in Gaza.

21. Repression of dissent in Israel, the right of access to information and treatment of human rights defenders

111. The Mission received reports that individuals and groups, viewed as sources of criticism of Israel's military operations were subjected to repression or attempted repression by the Government of Israel. Amidst a high level of support for the Israeli military operations in Gaza from the Israeli Jewish population, there were also widespread protests against the military operations inside Israel. Hundreds of thousands—mainly, but not exclusively, Palestinian citizens of Israel—protested. While

in the main, the protests were permitted to take place, there were occasions when, reportedly, protesters had difficulty in obtaining permits —particularly in areas populated mainly by Palestinian Israelis. 715 people in Israel and in occupied East Jerusalem were arrested during the protests. There appear to have been no arrests of counterprotesters and 34% of those arrested were under 18 years of age. The Mission notes that a relatively small proportion of those protesting were arrested. The Mission urges the Government of Israel to ensure that the police authorities respect the rights of all its citizens, without discrimination, including freedom of expression and right to peaceful assembly, as guaranteed to them by the ICCPR.

112. The Mission notes with concern the reported instances of physical violence against protesters committed by members of the police, including the beating of protester and other inappropriate conduct by the police including subjected Palestinian citizens of Israel who were arrested to racial abuse and making sexual comments about female members of their families. Article 10 of the ICCPR requires that those deprived of their liberty be treated with humanity and respect for the inherent dignity of the human person.

113. Of protesters brought before the Israeli courts, it was the Palestinian Israelis who were disproportionately held in detention pending trial. The element of discrimination and differential treatment between Palestinian and Jewish citizens of Israel by judicial authorities, as indicated in the reports received, is a substantial cause for concern.

114. The interviews of political activists by the Israeli General Security Services were cited as the actions contributing most significantly to a climate of repression inside Israel. The Mission is concerned about activists being compelled to attend interviews with Shabak, in the absence of any legal obligation to do so, and in general at the alleged interrogation of political activists about their political activities.

115. The Mission received reports concerning the investigation by the Government of Israel into New Profile on allegations that it was inciting draft-dodging, a criminal offence, and reports that the government was seeking to terminate funding from foreign governments for Breaking the Silence, following the group's publication of testimonies of Israeli soldiers concerning the conduct of Israeli military forces in Gaza in December 2008 and January 2009. The Mission is concerned that the Government of Israel's action with regard to these organizations may have an intimidating effect on other Israeli human rights organizations. The United Nations Declaration on Human Rights Defenders guarantees the right "to solicit, receive and utilise resources for the express purpose

of promoting and protecting human rights and fundamental freedoms through peaceful means". If motivated by reaction to the organisation's exercise of its freedom of expression, lobbying foreign governments to terminate funding would be contrary to the spirit of the Declaration.

116. The Government of Israel imposed a ban on media access to Gaza following 5 November 2008. Further, access was denied to human rights organizations and the ban continues for some international and Israeli organizations. The Mission can find no justifiable reason for this denial of access. The presence of journalists and international human rights monitors aides the investigation and wide public reporting of the conduct of the parties to the conflict and their presence can inhibit misconduct. The Mission observes that Israel, in its actions against political activists, NGOs and the media, has attempted to reduce public scrutiny of its conduct both during its military operations in Gaza and the consequences that these operations had for the residents of Gaza, possibly seeking to prevent investigation and public reporting thereon.

a. Accountability

22. Proceedings carried out or being carried out and responses by Israel to allegations of violations by security forces against Palestinians (Chapter XXV)

117. Investigations and, if appropriate, prosecutions of those suspected of serious violations are necessary steps if respect for human rights and humanitarian law is to be ensured and to prevent the development of a climate of impunity. States have a duty under international law to investigate allegations of violations.

118. The Mission reviewed public information and reports from the Government of Israel concerning actions taken to discharge its obligation to investigate alleged violations. It addressed to Israel a number of questions on this issue, but it did not receive a reply.

119. In response to allegations of serious violations of human rights law and international humanitarian law, the Military Advocate General ordered some criminal investigations that were closed two weeks later concluding that allegations "were based on hearsay". The Israeli armed forces also released the results of five special investigations carried out by high ranking military officers, which concluded that "throughout the fighting in Gaza, the IDF operated in accordance with international law", but the investigations reportedly revealed a very small number of errors. On 30 July 2009 the media reported that the Military Advocate General had ordered the Military Police to launch criminal investigations into

14 cases out or nearly 100 complaints of criminal conduct by soldiers. No details were offered.

120. The Mission reviewed the Israeli internal system of investigation and prosecution according to its national legislation and in the light of practice. The system comprises: a) disciplinary proceedings; b) operational debriefings (also known as "operational investigations,"); c) special investigations, performed by a senior officer at the request of the chief of staff; and d) Military Police investigations, carried out by the Criminal Investigation Division of the Military Police. At the heart of the system lays the so-called "operational debriefing". The debriefings are reviews of incidents and operations conducted by soldiers from the same unit or line of command together with a superior officer. They are meant to serve operational purposes.

121. International human rights law and humanitarian law require States to investigate and, if appropriate, prosecute allegations of serious violations by military personnel. International law has also established that such investigations should comply with standards of impartiality, independence, promptness and effectiveness. The Mission holds that the Israeli system of investigation does not comply with all those principles. In relation to the "operational debriefing" used by the Israeli armed forces as an investigative tool, the Mission holds the view that a tool designed for the review of performance and to learn lessons can hardly be an effective and impartial investigation mechanism that should be instituted after every military operation where allegations of serious violations have been made. It does not comply with internationally recognised principles of impartiality and promptness in investigations. The fact that proper criminal investigations can only start after the "operational debriefing" is over is a major flaw in the Israel system of investigation.

122. The Mission concludes that there are serious doubts about the willingness of Israel to carry out genuine investigations in an impartial, independent, prompt and effective way as required by international law. The Mission is also of the view that the Israeli system overall presents inherently discriminatory features that make the pursuit of justice for Palestinian victims very difficult.

23. Proceedings carried out or being carried out by Palestinian authorities (Chapter XXVI)

(a) Proceedings related to actions in the Gaza Strip

123. The Mission found no evidence of any system of public monitoring

or accountability for serious violations of international humanitarian law and human rights law set by the Gaza authorities. The Mission is concerned with the consistent disregard of international humanitarian law with which armed groups in the Gaza Strip conduct their armed activities, through rocket and mortar fire, directed against Israel. Despite some media reports, the Mission remains unconvinced that any genuine and effective initiatives have been taken by the authorities to address the serious issues of violation of IHL in the conduct of armed activities by militant groups in the Gaza Strip.

124. Notwithstanding statements by and any action that the Gaza authorities may have taken, and of which the Mission is unaware, the Mission also considers that allegations of killings, torture and mistreatment within the Gaza Strip have gone largely without investigation.

(b) Proceedings related to actions in the West Bank

125. With regard to relevant violations identified in the West Bank, with few exceptions, it appears that there has been a degree of tolerance towards human rights violations against political opponents, which has resulted in a lack of accountability for such actions. The Ministry of Interior has also ignored the High Court's decisions to release a number of detainees or to reopen some associations closed by the administration.

126. In the circumstances, the Mission is unable to consider the measures taken by the Palestinian Authority as significant for a meaningful accountability of those who have committed serious violations of international law and believes that the responsibility to protect the rights of the people inherent in the authority assumed by the PA must be fulfilled with greater commitment.

24. Universal jurisdiction

127. In the context of increasing unwillingness on the part of Israel to open criminal investigations that comply with international standards the Mission supports the reliance on universal jurisdiction as an avenue for States to investigate violations of the grave breach provisions of the Geneva Conventions of 1949, prevent impunity and promote international accountability (Chapter XXVIII).

25. Reparations

128. International law also establishes that whenever a violation of an

international obligation occur an obligation to provide reparation arises. It is the view of the Mission that the current constitutional structure and legislation in Israel leaves very limited room, if any, for Palestinians to seek compensation. It is necessary that the international community provides for an additional or alternative mechanism of compensation for damage or loss incurred by Palestinians civilians during the military operations (Chapter XXIX).

E. Conclusions and recommendations

129. The Mission draws general conclusions on the issues investigated in Chapter XXIX, which also includes a summary of its legal findings.

130. The Mission then makes recommendations to a number of United Nations bodies, Israel, responsible Palestinian authorities and the international community, in the areas of: (i) Accountability for serious violations of International Humanitarian Law; (b) Reparations; (c) Serious violations of human rights law; (d) The blockade and reconstruction; (e) The use of weapons and military procedures; (f) The protection of human rights organizations and defenders; (g) Follow up to the Mission's recommendations. The recommendations are detailed in Chapter XXX.

Gaza 2006 before Israeli Operation Cast Lead
of December 2008-January 2009

47

Hamas Government Building

Israeli forces deliberately killed 63 Palestinian police cadets attending their graduation ceremony

Search for bodies

Firefighters

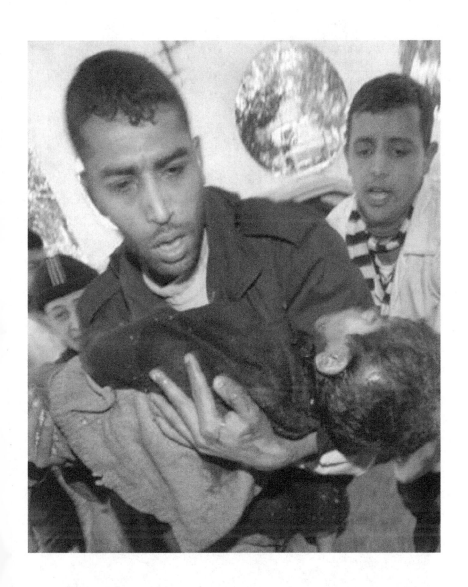

Palestinian Parliamentary Building

Bodies outtside UN school

UN Bullet-ridden school

Education Ministry

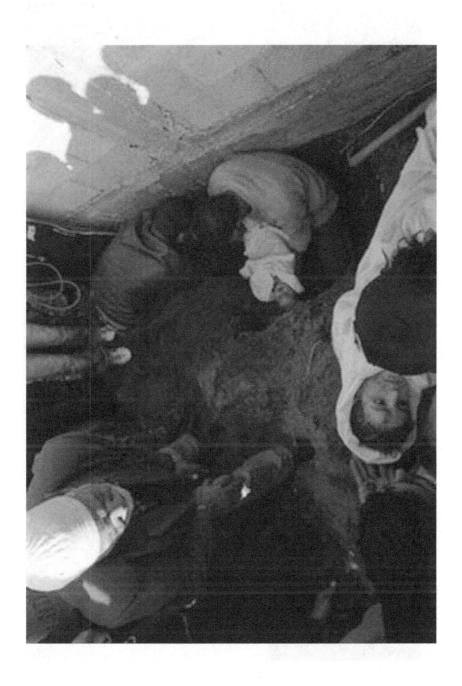

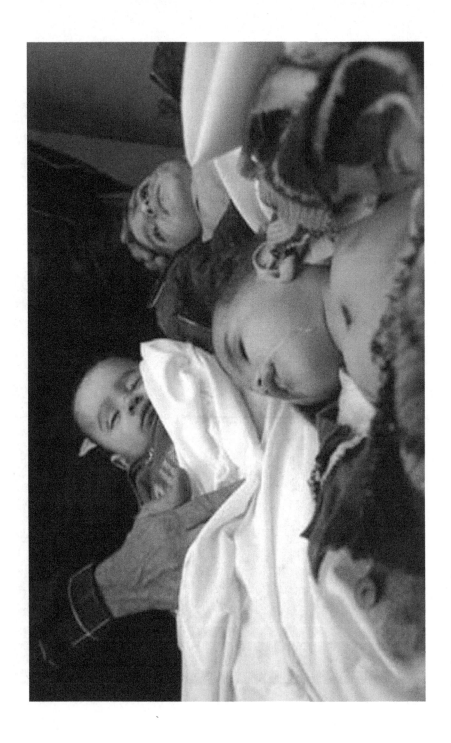

ON BENDED KNEES
ZIONIST POWER
IN AMERICAN POLITICS

"Obama wants to see a stop to settlements: Not some settlements, not outposts, not natural growth exceptions".
Secretary of State, Hillary Clinton, May 2009

*"What the prime minister [Netanyahu] has offered in specifics of a restraint on the policy of settlements... is unprecedented, **there has never been a precondition**, it's always been an issue within negotiations."*
Hillary Clinton, BBC, November 1, 2009
(my emphasis)

*"The US administration understands **what we have always said** ... that the real obstacle to negotiations is the Palestinians (calling for a freeze on settlements)".*
Daniel Hershkowitz
Israeli Minister of Science and Technology
November 1, 2009 (my addition).

"America, stop sucking up to Israel!"
Gideon Levy, Israeli journalist,
Haaretz, November 1, 2009.

"US Zionists are sticking it to America, 24/7",
Anonymous Staff Official, Washington D. C.
October 31, 2009.

Introduction

The discussion of Zionist Power Configuration (ZPC) in the US political system revolves around several essential issues, including:

1) The claims by the ZPC that it *represents* Jewish opinion and values as well as has its authority to speak for the interests of the American people.

2) Measuring the power of the ZPC and determining its influence over policy, appointments and political institutions.

3) The question of whether the ZPC is a legitimate part of the US political system, another lobby, or something very different, an unregistered agent of a foreign power (Israel).

4) The scope and depth of the ZPC influence in US politics beyond the focus on its "lobbying" in Washington on a "single issue".

5) The organizational weapons and techniques utilized by the ZPC to maximize influence and deny voice and influence to critics of Israel and itself.

6) The similarities of the organizational linkages of the US Israel-Zionist relationship to those of the Russian Stalinist-Communist Parties of the 1930s.

Sources: Public Records, Ethnic Neutral Sources and Citations

The case against the Zionist Power Configuration is based on the *open record* of publications, speeches, articles, interviews and sources available to the general public (and any interested reader). Many facts and data are drawn from Zionist and Israeli sources as well as mainstream publications and writings by critical journalists and analysts.[1] We should not *privilege* the statements by Jews, whether they are critics or supporters of the State of Israel, as most "progressive" writers do. The pursuit of truth is not an "ethnic science", an approach that smacks of Nazi and Zionist racial theories. Indeed, nothing reveals the extreme Zionist power or cultural hegemony over the debate on Israel and American Zionism so much as the constant reliance, reference and citation of the "Jewish" authorship of critical articles, even when publications by non-Jews are better documented, of earlier publication, and better argued.

The ethnic (Jewish) label attached to writings and intellectual and political activity is *selectively* applied: the ethnic labels are applied to 'positive outcomes' as part of a general campaign exalting the "superiority" of the "race"; and disregarded in the face of 'negative outcomes' and activities (e.g. financial swindles, Russian oligarchs, espionage agents). In fact the "double standard" is buttressed by savage attacks by the ZPC on those who, following the ethnic labeling tradition, actually mention the Jewish background of mediocrities and war criminals as well as that of peace and justice advocates.

We will begin by questioning and challenging the *representativeness* of the ZPC in the United States today.

Zionists as Representative of the Jewish Communities in America

The Conference of Presidents of the Major American Jewish Organization (PMAJO) claims to speak for *all* Jews in the US.[2] A major study in the north Boston region found that less than 25% of Jews belong to a synagogue, even fewer (10%) contribute to the Jewish Federations of North America and over 50% do not accept rabbinical Zionist precepts against inter-marriage with non-Jews.[3] According to the Jewish Telegraph Agency (12/4/2009) conservative synagogues have declined by almost 25% from 800 to 650 over the past decade. Even more striking, many prominent individuals who may be of Jewish parentage, no longer consider themselves "Jews" despite frequent claims by Zionists that their achievements are a product or a result of their being "Jewish". Near majorities of young people of Jewish ancestry do not identify with Judaism and are critical or indifferent to Zionist appeals for Israel. They have no involvement in Jewish centered civic activities.[4] A small but vocal group of Jews are organized and active critics of the entire Zionist apparatus, rejecting the idea of Israel as an exclusive ethno-religious state and supporting a secular democratic republic in Palestine.[5] In addition several Orthodox Jewish sects view the 'state of Israel' as a form of blasphemy and call for its destruction.[6]

The "51" misrepresent their actual numbers and claim to speak for 6 million US Jews. At best they may speak for less than half of the imputed population and even then their support waxes and wanes according to the issue, the timing and the place and varies in intensity. The power of the "51" is *not* a result of its representativeness of the Jewish community at large, but the *location* of its followers in the power structure and the intensity and quasi-religious fervor of their activists. Their political power resides in their singular forces in pursuit of the interests of the State of Israel; their control and influence in media; their nationwide networks and the wealth and financial power of contributors. Their capacity to browbeat apathetic Jews into making contributions and lending support adds organizational muscle. Their willing use of force, money and media slander intimidates any and all critics, including dissident politicians, media, journalists and professors.[7]

At most there are probably no more than 500,000 Jews who actively back the "51"—but what a half million! Given the low level of political participation of the US population in general, the relatively low saliency of Middle East issues for most Americans and the one-sided pro-Israel mass media propaganda, which misinforms the public, the Zionist zealots have little competition. They have a free hand in penetrating and influencing political, social and cultural institutions in line with the policies dictated by their Israeli-influenced leaders among the "51".

The issue of the limited *representativeness* of the Zionist organization must be separated from their *exercise of power*. By leveraging non-Zionist, non-Jewish civic organizations, political institutions, pension funds, trade unions, etc. the ZPC magnifies its power beyond its numbers.[8]

The limited *representativeness* of the "51" is compensated by the silence and apathy of the majority of Jews and "non-Jewish" Jews, who either are not willing to challenge ZPC claims or are immersed in private concerns, careers or other unrelated civic issues.

The '51's hundreds of thousands of activists are *strategically* placed in institutions, as well as *geographically*, with a centralized command capable of mobilizing money, media attention and political leverage in any priority, political, cultural or social arena[9]. The '51' organizations are not merely a "lobby" in the sense of having paid officials operating to influence congressional votes.[10] They include religious, civic, charitable, ideological, cultural and social organizations unified and unconditionally committed to following the zigzags of Israeli political directives.[11] The actual structure resembles a 'power configuration' that reaches from small chapters in municipalities to statewide confederations as well as national organizations, each with its own budget, its own ideological watchdogs and appropriate levels of power.

The mobilization of power for Israel is exercised by elected and appointed Zionist officials, especially those in positions that have any relevance to Israeli interests. These "interests" include the promotion of direct aid to Israel, sanctions and wars against Israel's Middle East and Asian adversaries, American pension fund investments in Israel, boycotts of companies trading with Israeli-designated adversary countries and many other strategic concerns.

The *key* to the power of the Zionist Power Configuration is that it is a *mass grassroots organization*, bolstered by the financial support of scores of millionaires, dozens of billionaires and a complicit mass media. These political resources translate into tremendous leverage over the far more numerous non-Zionist electorates, the mass media spectators and the upwardly mobile politicians.

The ZPC illustrates clearly how "numbers" in the abstract do not count,[12] especially in a permeable electoral system like that of the US, where money, organization, discipline and ethno-religious fanaticism define the boundaries, issues and acceptable policies.

ZPC/Congress Dismiss the *Goldstone Report*

The recent decision of the US Congress (HR 867) to repudiate the findings of Israeli war crimes in the official *Final Report of the United Nations' Fact Finding Mission on the 2009 Gaza Conflict* by a vote of 344–36 is a measure of the power of the ZPC.[13] The report, also known as the *"Goldstone Report"*, after its principal author, Justice Richard Goldstone, was released on September 15, 2009, amid a carefully orchestrated campaign to discredit its findings and its authors. What is even more important than the US Congressional vote of condemnation is the fact that the campaign was publically ordered from Israel, directed by the 51 Presidents and obediently and enthusiastically carried out by several hundred thousand Zionist activists, throughout the country. The '51' and the mass of Zionist zealots were openly defending Israeli state terror and crimes against humanity. That they were defending war crimes never evoked a second thought. What mattered was their ability to pressure, threaten, cajole and promise future funds to Congressional representatives in order to secure their vote against Justice Goldstone's *Report*. Blind obedience to Israeli dictates was evident in the fact that many Congresspersons proudly confessed to never having even read the *Goldstone Report* and that none dared question the egregious fabrications, which its two uber-Zionist Congressional sponsors of HR 867, (Representatives H.L. Berman, D-California and G.L. Ackermann, D-New York, concocted.[14] The US Congress, in fact, almost unanimously rejected the eminent Justice Goldstone's request to present his findings in person.

In the UN General Assembly, the Zionists were able to leverage the US to vote against the *Goldstone Report*, which in turn secured the vote of several Eastern European client states, insignificant island dependencies and the predictable Western European "Allies". This amounted to a total of 18 votes *against* the 114 UN members who endorsed the *Report*'s thorough documentation of Israeli war crimes and state terrorism, an endorsement which represented over 80% of the world's population.[15]

The ZPC is powerful but not *omnipotent*. It controls the US Congress and Executive and has decisive influence in the mass media, but there are important fissures in the monolith, as a number of Jewish organizations and individuals, revolted by Israel's mass killings in Gaza and the ZPC unconditional support for same, have spoken out in support of the *Goldstone Report*.[16] More importantly, major national trade/union federations in Canada, Ireland, Great Britain, France and Italy, along with numerous human rights organizations, support a global boycott and disinvestment campaign against Israeli products.[17] Judicial processes are proceeding in various European countries to arrest and put on trial top Israeli officials involved in the Gaza massacre.[18]

The United States, under the tutelage of the ZPC, remains as the center of Israeli power and the sole reliable backer of Israeli war aims in the Middle East, especially with regard to Iran. The power of Israel over Washington's Middle East policy is in direct relation to the strategic influence of the ZPC. The *denial* of the power of the ZPC by seemingly "*progressive*" and "*leftist*" writers and journalists has been one of the principal obstacles undermining efforts to effectively counter US government support for Israeli war crimes, the expansion of colonial settlements in the West Bank and the military/sanctions policies toward Iran.[19]

Israeli Power over US Middle East Policy: The Centrality of the ZPC

The manifestations of Israeli power over the US are public, visible, outrageous and unprecedented in the annals of US foreign relations.[20] Israeli power is wielded directly through its subordinated political arm, the ZPC, which in turn facilitates the *direct intervention* of the Israeli state in the internal politics of the US. Let us examine several crucial *empirical* indicators of Israeli power in the US.

On November 9, 2009, Israeli Prime Minister Benjamin Netanyahu addressed the mass based Jewish Federation (JF) of North America General Assembly and thanked US President Obama and the US Congress for repudiating the *Goldstone Report*. The Israeli head of state then told his US followers to increase their efforts to influence US policy to "stop Teheran from realizing its nuclear ambitions".[21] The previous day, Israel's Ambassador to the United States, Michael Oren, told the same Jewish Federation to "press for sanctions on Iran and condemn the findings of the United Nations Commission on Gaza.[22] Speaking as a tribal chieftain dictating orders to the loyal overseas followers, Oren stated, "Our strength derives from the belief that we have a right to independence in our tribal land, the land of Israel..."[23] Israel is the only country that can intervene in the internal politics of the US, counting on a powerful political organization, to shape US policy to serve its state interests.

Drawing on the now discredited myth that American Jews' tribal ancestry is rooted in Israel, rather than in Khazaria in Central Asia, reinforces the idea that Israel—and not the United States—is the true 'homeland' of American Jews and therefore it is their right and duty to obey the dictates of the Israeli state.[24] Each year dozens of Israeli state officials visit the US and directly intervene in US political debates, congressional hearings and executive policy making—with nary a whisper of protest, let alone censure from the US State Department. Any other country's officials who so flagrantly intervene in US politics would be declared *persona non grata* and expelled from the country. In contrast, because of the power of the ZPC, Israeli civilians and military officials are *invited* to intervene in US policy making, to set the agenda for numerous Zionist officials in and out of public office and to bludgeon and praise those who criticize or oppose Israeli dictates.[25] The repeated public statements by Israeli officials that the primary loyalty of American Jews is to Israel and its policies—in other words, that they should act as what would otherwise be widely understood and recognized as a fifth column for Israel—is incompatible with the notion of citizenship everywhere except for this small group in the US.[26] One could imagine the outcry (and brutal reprisals) if any political leader from a Muslim country called on their co-religionists to pursue its state interests. What is striking then about the ZPC is that it *openly* and *publicly* organizes meetings, follows orders and pursues policies dictated by Israeli public officials and yet is not registered as a *foreign agent*, let alone prosecuted for acting, by its own admission, on behalf of a foreign power.[27]

The ZPC: A Lobby or Unregistered Foreign Agents?

Based on its organizational structure and political aims, the pro-Israel social-political configuration cannot be reduced to a common "lobby". The mass activist organizational structure *encompassing* and *penetrating* civic, political, cultural institutions and media outlets resembles a power configuration that works within and outside of Washington to shape political decisions relevant to Israel.[28] Equally important it plays a major role in shaping the opinions and behavior of public opinion and civic society organizations. Secondly, unlike American lobbies, it acts to shape US foreign policy *in the interest* of a foreign military power, up to and including decisions on promoting war and imposing sanctions against Israel's opponents, prejudicing the lives and security of thousands of American working people and taxpayers. Thirdly, the term "lobby" does not ordinarily encompass the virulent repressive activities pursued by the ZPC against critical writers, cultural figures, academics and others in American society who question Israeli policy. The ZPC not only acts a foreign agent for Israel today, but has been openly doing so for over fifty years.[29] In the 1960s the Justice Department attempted to enforce the 1938 *Foreign Agents Registration Act (FARA)* against the current American Israel Public Affairs Committee (AIPAC)'s predecessor, the American Zionist Council (AZC), but was blocked by pro-Israel politicians.

The ZPC not only publically gives unconditional support to Israeli policy but engages in *espionage* on behalf of Israel as several prominent members of the ZPC and Mossad have testified. One of America's leading experts on Israel's "lobby", Grant Smith, has amassed a vast archive of declassified official US documents on Israeli-Zionist activities in the US. He cites numerous cases in which AIPAC purloined internal classified government documents in order to further Israeli trade privileges in the 1980s.[30] A leader of the Zionist Organization of America was implicated in the illegal transfer of US government uranium to Israel in 1956. In 2005 Steve Rosen and Keith Weissman, leaders in AIPAC, admitted to receiving a confidential document relating to US-Iran policy, and transmitting it to an Israeli embassy official.[31] From 1979 to 1985, senior US Army weapons engineer Ben-ami Kadish, an American Zionist and former member of the fanatical Jewish Haganah militia in British Mandate Palestine, handed critical confidential documents on an enormous number of US weapons systems over to agents from the Israeli embassy.[32] These were then believed to have been passed to the

Soviet Union in order to influence their policy on immigration to Israel. Under the influence of the Zionist-infested Justice Department, Kadish got off with a $50,000 fine and not a single day in jail—for handing scores of crucial US military secrets to Israel.

Ben-ami Kadish's fellow spy, American Zionist Jonathan Pollard, shared the same Mossad handler in the 1980s. Pollard, who worked as an analyst for US Naval intelligence, provided the Israelis with crate-loads of classified military and intelligence documents filled with top secret information on US policy in the Middle East, weapons systems, US agents in the Soviet Union, and any and all relevant strategic objects of interest to his Israeli handlers.[33]

On October 29, 2009, the Justice Department charged Stewart David Nozette, a Defense Department scientist, with attempting to transmit classified information to an Israeli Mossad agent. Nozette, an American Zionist, did not act strictly out of tribal loyalties to the Jewish State. Like Pollard, he asked for money and an Israeli passport.[34] According to former Mossad agent Victor Ostrovsky, the spy agency recruits thousands of overseas Zionist *sayanim* (Hebrew for 'helpers') who "must be 100 percent Jewish" for Israeli Mossad operations, which may include terrorism.[35] In 2001 Fox News investigative reporter, Carl Cameron, reported that scores of Israeli spies were rounded up and deported in the aftermath of 9/11, including five Mossad agents videoing the World Trade Center bombing.[36]

Industrial and political spying is not uncommon among states, even between allies. What is striking is that representatives of an organized ethno-religious group, the major American Zionist organizations, have expressed sympathy and solidarity with such spies as Ben-ami Kadish, Jonathan Pollard and others, even defending their acts of espionage as a significant contribution to US-Israeli relations.[37] The implication, or better still, the explication for this perverse thinking is that for the leading American Zionist organizations, spying for Israel is part and parcel of their primary loyalty to the Jewish state. Zionist primary loyalty to Israel is not confined to mainline American Jewish organizations.

During the Rosen-Weissman trial, numerous prominent Jewish leftists (including *Democracy Now's* Amy Goodman) publicly defended the procuring of confidential documents and *their handing over to a foreign (Israeli) government* as a matter of "free speech" and "freedom of the press".[38] Rosen in his civil suit against his firing by AIPAC (to deflect FBI investigators) claimed that his handing over of US government documents to Israeli officials was "*common practice*" for AIPAC officials.[39]

Top Zionist leaders in the Bush and Obama administration have a long history of working for and with Israel, including in some cases, activity which has caused them to lose security clearances and/or to come under investigation.[40] Two top Pentagon officials in the Bush administration, Former Undersecretary of Defense Paul Wolfowitz and Assistant Secretary of Defense, Douglas Feith are cases in point. Obama's chief of staff, Rahm Emmanuel, spent time in the Israeli armed forces and has long been suspected of ties to Mossad.[41] Stuart Levey, a top US Treasury Department official involving in enforcing sanctions against Iran, has spent nearly a decade in close collaboration with MOSSAD, a point he brags about.[42] During the Bush (Jr.) Presidency, non-Zionist officials in the Pentagon and CIA complained of being sidelined by top Zionist officials, who set up their own intelligence offices run by their own fellow Zionist policymakers.[43] Wolfowitz and Feith set up the Pentagon's Office of Special Plans run by Abram Shulsky. Colonel Karen Kwiatkowski, an official in the Pentagon at the time, complained of being marginalized and supplanted by Israeli officers who had unfettered access to the highest Pentagon officials.[44] The November 2007 *United States National Intelligence Estimate Report* (NIE) on the Iranian nuclear program was savaged by all the major Jewish American organizations, and their cohorts in Congress and the Executive branch because the report concluded that Iran had suspended its nuclear weapons development since 2003.[45] The major Zionist organizations and their supporters in the US government favored Israeli intelligence disinformation claiming an active nuclear weapons program that threatened US security. In short order the *NIE* report, prepared by 16 major US Government intelligence agencies, was pushed aside and US policy followed the lead of the Zionist-backed Israeli claims of a "secret" Iranian weapons program despite the absence of any hard data.

Leveraging Power

The key to Zionist power in shaping US policy toward the Mid-East, Arab-Muslim relations and toward "third parties" affecting Israeli policy is the *combined* influence of Zionists in executive offices (Treasury, State, National Security, Pentagon, etc.) and Congress, especially leading committees relevant to Israeli interests, as well as the mass organizations in civil society (the '51' major American Jewish organizations) and Zionist control over the mass media.[46] Zionist power and control in these crucial areas spreads out into influencing academic activity, including the repression of Israeli critics, the censoring of publications, manipulation of professional societies, trade unions and state and union pension funds, whose members are overwhelmingly neither Jewish nor Zionist.

The result is that the Zionist Power Configuration's automatic and unquestioning *support* for the crimes and treason, including Zionist espionage for Israel within the US and the universally-condemned

Israel war crimes, goes uncontested in the mass media, the Congress, and even by the small political and literary journals on the 'Left'. This uncontested support of espionage by a foreign power acting through public organizations is unique in US history. In the past organizations acting as surrogates for a foreign power were condemned, ostracized, suppressed, prosecuted and subject to mass public outrage. It is a "tribute" to the power of ZPC that none of that occurs today. As a footnote to history, this is the first time that practically all Marxist journals, monthlies, bi-monthlies, quarterlies and annuals and their leading contributors have avoided a serious critique of the ZPC. On the contrary, the sparse articles which purport to deal with Middle East policies cover-up the role of the ZPC in shaping US policy.[47]

There is evidence that, even in the most radical publications of "critical writing", fellow traveling editors, who otherwise claim "internationalist" and "working class" allegiances, are not willing to confront the ZPC war makers who promote wars in the Middle East, funded by *American* taxpayers and fought by 99.9% *non Jewish/non-Zionist working class Americans* in uniform.

The Interlocking Directorate: Establishing Zionist Hegemony

Several critical analysts have identified some of the key issues and institutions under Zionist influence.[48] Some have identified AIPAC as an influential pro-Israel lobby. Others have noted the pro-Israel bias of the mass media.[49] A very few have even identified Zionist predominance in media ownership.[50]

Others, especially during the Bush presidency, noted the influence of key Zionists in the Pentagon, especially their role in promoting the US invasion of Iraq.[51] The narrow focus of their otherwise valuable critiques fails to account for *structural continuities* over time and place: the long-term, large-scale presence of unconditional *Israel Fisters* across administrations especially over the past two decades. Moreover, while case studies of Zionist influence over specific policy issues, such as the recent Congressional repudiation of the Goldstone Report and support for Israeli war crimes, are useful, the larger theoretical and empirical phenomenon of the growing *chain of issues* over ever more extended policy areas of interest to Israel (and therefore the ZPC) is ignored.[52] In a word, the problem of ZPC power in the US is not confined to a *single issue lobby*. This narrow approach obfuscates the systemic role of the ZPC in effectively disenfranchising the great majority of the American wage and salaried people (at the expense of their living standards), increasing war taxes for the middle class and blocking investment opportunities for corporate America in countries designated (by Israel) as "security threats" (adversaries of Israeli colonial expansion).

The career patterns of leading Zionists include movers and shakers from business (Wall Street, Corporate law firms) to government; another pattern involves Zionist academics who move to the executive branch and then on to corporate or Zionist think tanks. Others follow a career combining academic/propagandist/journalist policy consultant positions, often prominent on the television political 'talk' shows. The leading media moguls combine roles as CEOs, propagandists, and Israel advocates. The overlap of career positions creates a network of *shared* ideologies, defined by 'what is best for Israel' (*Israel First*). The shared "world view" creates a cohesive group that sets the boundaries of US policy debate. Congressional behavior, Executive policy makers and intellectual discourse are confined by these ZPC-determined parameters. In effect pro-Israel career patterns and projections of power have established a kind of Judeo-Zionist hegemony of US public life.

Ethnicizing Truth

One of the extreme manifestations of Zionist-Jewish hegemony is the fear and trepidation with which critics of Israeli policy approach the issue. Most seek to "*Judaize*" any criticism, instead of seeking and citing truth, facts or analyses on their own merits. They support their statements by citing *Israeli* sources and *Jewish* writers, even if earlier non-Jewish, non-Israeli writers and analysts have raised the same issues and may have provided a more systematic and consequential critique.[53] This "tactic" of seeking to foreground *critical* Jews to stave off attacks by the ZPC and Israel is *debatable* if not counter-productive, regressive and serves to re-enforce the pervasive fear of the ZPC. The proponents of this approach, assuming they are not ignorant of non-Jewish critics, argue that by citing the Jewish background of the critics of Israel, they disarm the ZPC charge of "anti-Semitism". They further argue that by putting an ethnic 'spin' or 'ethnicizing' the critique they are responding to "Jewish sensibilities" and are more likely to get a hearing from Jews and their sympathizers.[54]

These arguments are both understandable and plausible *but* deeply flawed. Committed Zionists, meaning the entire ZPC, dismiss Jewish and non-Jewish critics with equal ferocity: the former as "self-hating Jews", the latter as "anti-Semites". Sacrificing truth and principled criticism to shield "Jewish sensibilities" means refraining from challenging their residual tribal sympathies to a 'Zion-centric' view of the world. If the central problem is Zionist hegemony over US culture and especially foreign policy in the Middle East (and wherever else Israel dictates), it ill behooves us to pander to amorphous '*special sensitivities*' of the few Jewish dissidents who demand ethnically-based critiques.

Demystifying a Racial Doctrine

The big challenge for opponents of Judeo-Zionist hegemony is demystifying its ideological bases. Zionists and their media camp followers always *highlight* "Jewishness" and the disproportionate number of notable, successful scientists and public figures with whom the Zionists self-identify (even if the said individuals, themselves, have no sense of identification with anything remotely "Jewish" beyond some distant ancestry). In contrast, to highlight the "Jewishness" (and Israel-centricity) of notorious swindlers, spies, warmongers, gangsters, drug or arms traffickers is be labeled anti-Semitic. *Selective* ethnic identity is crucial to maintaining and perpetuating the racist myth of Jewish *superiority* and its corollary of power and prestige, based on *special meritorious qualities.* One of the key components of Zionist-Jewish ideology and Israeli power is precisely the racist myth of the Jewish moral and intellectual superiority—not the guns, money and backing of Washington and the ZPC's central location within the US elite social structure.

There are *two options* for those interested in demystifying the notion of Zionist-Jewish superiority: *One could eliminate all ethnic labels or one could insist that labels be applied to all individuals including the most nefarious, grotesque and embarrassing.*

Despite cracks in the Zionist monolith and the emergence of public critics within and without the Jewish community,[55] especially among young former Jews, who prefer to assimilate into a secular albeit Anglo-Americanized majority with their fellow-citizens (the *passive* majority), still up to a third of US Jews remain hard-core *backers* of the ZPC with Israel as their most *enduring* political loyalty. While not discounting the *psychological* gratifications that accompany beliefs in a mythical biblical past, there are *real material benefits* to joining the Israel First Power Configuration. While it is true Zionists *contribute* money and time to promoting the Israeli agenda, there are also powerful material incentives, especially the benefits accruing from exclusive identification with and membership in a cohesive elite configuration, which empowers its members, finances electoral campaigns and is well-connected among political leaders, as well as financial, real estate and insurance moguls. The spinoffs and payoffs for upwardly mobile Zionist activists can be lucrative and career-enhancing. Ambitious politicians, who measure up and toe the line, are likely to tap into substantial funding and favorable media coverage. Networks that work for Israel enhance Jewish-Zionist prestige while providing emotional gratification and vicarious pleasure in *sharing the thrill* of Israel's bloody military victories and its forceful expansion of the "fatherland". Not a few careers have advanced through the "contacts" made at the national and regional Zionist meetings. This is especially the case for many, otherwise mediocre, political candidates facing competitive elections. Active membership in a powerful Zionist organization may protect the careers of lackluster, or even incompetent, performers in some academic or professional settings where the threat of a lawsuit charging anti-Semitism can ensure contract renewal.

Zionist racist ideology, with its implicit and explicit emphasis on Jews as "special people" ordained by God, as well as the media's bias toward presenting a selectively *positive* ethno-religious identity, provides symbolic gratification to lower middle class Jews, who sell Israel bonds, write letters to politicians, heckle critics of the Jewish state and march under the flag of Israel. They are likely to play a role at the grassroots level in bullying family members, neighbors and colleagues to join the cause or refrain from voicing criticism of Israel. Recently, more than a few Seders have led to family bust-ups over issues like the massacre of Palestinian civilians in Gaza, the *Goldstone Report* and the Ben-ami Kadish spy episode.

The success of the ZPC in projecting power and shaping US policy depends, in large part, on the financial clout of its millionaire financiers, its penetration of the state apparatus and the interlock of the corporate-political directorate. However, equally important is the grassroots work of hundreds of thousands of middle and lower middle class activists. The effective exercise of power by the Zionist elites is based on the vertical ties between the leaders and followers, especially in mobilizing for Israel's *high priority* campaigns promoting dubious causes—like Israeli repudiation of moderate US policies toward Jewish colonial settler expansion or calls for *more restraint* from killing civilians in Palestine and elsewhere. It is highly unlikely that any changes can be induced among the Zionist elite; but there are reasons to believe that some sections of the rank and file can be influenced by anti-Zionist Jews and non-Jews. This is especially true at a time when Israeli political leaders have embraced such openly ultra-rightist postures.

Zionist Hegemony Is Vulnerable

Several developments encourage the hope that these vertical links can be weakened. Over the past 5 years, numerous articles, books and videos critical of Israel have broken through Zionist censorship. Equally important, the emergence of new activist Jewish anti-Zionist organizations and the vast increase in member organizations supporting a boycott and divestment campaign against Israeli products, companies and cultural institutions have broken the ZPC stranglehold on public opinion.[56] Faced with growing opposition in civil society, the ZPC has escalated its *repressive efforts* to ban publication of critical authors, fire academics and savage journalists and politicians.[57] Simultaneously a concerted effort has been made to encourage its ideological 'attack dogs' in academia to suppress *any* critical discussion of the issues that most discredit the Israeli state, namely the recent Israeli massacres in Gaza, the brutal expansion of settlements in the West Bank, the *Goldstone Report* on Israeli war crimes and Israel's well-orchestrated push for war against Iran.[58]

Zionist Intellectuals: In Defense of Terror

The ZPC has long established a near stranglehold on the major media outlets for opinion and analysis on the Middle East and especially on issues, which Israel's foreign office has given high priority. As a result *Israel First* academics and pundits monopolize the editorial and opinion pages of the *Washington Post*, the Murdoch chain, the *Wall Street Journal*, *The New York Times*, the *Los Angeles Times*, the *Chicago Tribune*, *Newsweek*, and other print outlets.[59] The spread of Zionist extremism is evident in two recent feature articles published by *Newsweek* (December 21, 2009), glorifying Meir Dagan the neo-fascist head of the Israeli secret police, Mossad, for his success in assassinating political adversaries in violation of national boundaries and for his close ties with US Treasury official and Zionist zealot Stuart Levey, who is in charge of blackmailing Iran's trade and investment partners, in order to strangle the Iranian economy and impoverish seventy million of its people. The *Newsweek* authors of these articles are rightwing Israel and US Zionists.

Notorious Zionist news anchors, like Ted Koppel and Wolf Blitzer, parrot the Israeli-ZPC line in the major media (Fox News, CBS, NBC, ABC, CNN, BBC) as well as secondary outlets (National "*Public*" Radio).[60] The result is a plethora of self-styled "experts" of dubious loyalty to the America, but with strong ties to Israel and Zionist propaganda institutes, who grind out opinion pieces which defend the Israeli regime's most atrocious war crimes and land grabs.[61] Numerous professors from the most prestigious universities hack out op-ed pieces defending Israel's assault on Gaza, fabricating judicial precedents, and citing "Just War" theory.[62]

Israeli Prime Minister Benyamin Netanyahu, when confronted by near universal support for the *Goldstone Report*, ordered the ZPC to denigrate Justice Goldstone, the basis and legality of the *Report* and falsify its contents. When the extreme militarists, like Netanyahu, passed the word to Israel's mouthpieces in North America, they unleashed the ZPC's entire stable of academics, journalists and propagandists. Over one hundred op-ed pieces in the major media savaged the Report, slandered Goldstone and defended Israeli terror attacks, which destroyed the entire human infrastructure of the Gaza.[63] No Israeli crime was too great to cause any Harvard, Yale, Princeton or John Hopkins Zionist academic to rethink their blind subordination to the

Jewish state. They parroted Netanyahu's line that the massacre over one thousand civilians and the brutalization of hundreds of thousands was an exercise of *"Israel's right to self-defense"*. Those few of the Jewish and non-Jewish academics, who dared to criticize Israel's terrorist policy, cited the weakest section of the *Goldstone Report*—its amalgamating Israel's all-out terror bombing of Palestinian neighborhoods, schools, hospitals, mosques and farms, with Hamas' futile and ineffective retaliatory rockets falling mostly on empty Israeli fields. Few if any raised their voices against the *domestic* propaganda arm of Israeli war crimes—the Presidents of the 51 Major Jewish American Organizations. Needless to say, with few domestic critics willing to even *identify* their opponents, the ZPC secured over 90% of the US Congress in favor of Israel's repudiations of the *Goldstone Report*, which they had never even read.[64]

What is striking about the vast majority of Zionist academic apologists of terrorism is their shoddy scholarship, their tendentious and illogical arguments and de-contextualized analogies. Their 'persuasiveness' is based on the fact that their 'line' is *reinforced* by the mass media and *enforced* by the ZPC's political thuggery and character assassination of potential critics. Their repeated presence in the media gives the appearance of legitimacy in defending violations of international law. Their prestigious positions provide a veneer of expertise or knowledge even as their research in the region is based on flawed premises, including disproven religious legends and colonial mythology.[65] As Zionist academics become more deeply involved in justifying the expansionist Zionist claims, Israeli conquests and brutal militarism there is an accompanying marked deterioration of intellectual standards. Over time prestigious positions become linked with mediocrity. Academic degrees, awards and badges of merit are harnessed to hack writing and political hatchet jobs. Noted critics, who exempt Israeli war crimes and terror, are still published by prestigious publishers, despite their shabby intellectual output. Promotions and academic chairs are secured by eminently distinguished apologists of dubious morality. Their blind support and defense of the practices of a terror state puts the lie to their claims to high ethical and scholarly standards.

The American Zionist academic elite fits Adorno's authoritarian personality: at *the throat of the American polity and at the feet of the Israeli-ZPC elite*.[66] Arrogant posturing, angry polemics and emotional ejaculations cover up for their lack of substantive arguments. Where bullying fails, soothing rhetoric which speaks to values, dialogue and cooperation accompanies a blind eye to the relentless Israeli uprooting of Arab residents from Palestinian/Jerusalem. Princeton academics cite classical political theorists in defense of gun-toting Jewish settlers who brutalize shepherds, threaten school girls and up-root centuries-old Palestinian olive groves.

The Globalization of Zionist Power

From the Israeli fatherland to the nerve centers of Zionist power in the US, using the experiences and drawing on the support of the ZPC, pro-Israel influence has spread to important political institutions in England, Canada, France, Netherlands, Russia and more recently South America. In England, leaders and deputies from both the Conservative and Labor party accept millions in campaign funds from billionaire Zionists, paid junkets to Israel and other payoffs in exchange for supporting Israel's most egregious acts of violence in Lebanon, Gaza and the West Bank.[67] Zionist front groups like the "Conservative Friends (*flunkeys*) of Israel" and "Labor Friends (*flunkeys*) of Israel" ensure that the incumbent regimes and the opposition put Israeli trade and militarist interests at the center of British Middle East Policy.[68]

In Canada under the Conservative Harper regime, Zionists have secured unprecedented influence and diplomatic and material support for Israel's top priorities.[69] These include support for the annexation of most of Palestinian East Jerusalem; repudiation of the *Goldstone Report;* support for Israeli war crimes during the 2008/09 invasion of Gaza; Israel's invasion of Lebanon and pending legislations criminalizing criticism of Zionism as "anti-Semitism" among a host of other pro-Israel acts, decrees and trade privileges. The opposition Liberal and New Democratic parties compete with the Conservatives in pandering to the pro-Israel power configurations in order to secure campaign financing from millionaire real estate, financial and media moguls. In contrast, major Canadian trade unions and anti-Zionist Jewish campus and community organizations have organized boycotts of Israeli goods and academic organizations serving the bloody occupation. In France, life-long Zionist zealot, Foreign Minister Bernard "Bernie" Kouchner, has embraced Netanyahu's extreme position of "unconditional negotiations" which allows massive land seizures and the construction of '*Jews-only*' apartment complexes on illegally confiscated Palestinian land to continue while endless inconsequential "peace" negotiations take place.[70] This position has been supported by Uber-Zionist Secretary of State, Hillary Clinton.

In Russia, following the collapse of the Soviet Union, eight of the top nine billionaire oligarchs claimed dual Israeli citizenship. They illegally and violently seized hundreds of billions of dollars worth of formerly state-owned mines, factories and banks, and then transferred part of their illicit fortunes to overseas banks in Israel, the US, London and the money-laundering offshore island states and tax-havens. Zionist power peaked during the debauched Presidency of Yeltsin in the 1990s, but residual influence is evident in the Putin-Mevedev regime. This is particularly apparent in the US- Russian accords to increase sanctions on Iran, a policy that jeopardizes billions of dollars in Russian investments and trade with Iran.

Russia has resolutely refused to pressure Israel over its colonial settlement expansion. In a similar manner, Israel retains a decisive influence over Holland and Germany's Middle East policy, via the exploitation of the Holocaust Memory, the Ann Frank legacy and the pressure of pro-Israel economic sectors.

The newest example of the "globalization" of Zionist power and the drive for new Israeli spheres of influence is found in Latin America. Major US Zionist organizations have contributed substantial financial resources to building, advising and orienting their counterparts, especially in Argentina, Brazil and Peru, while engaging in a systematic effort to curry favor with the US by demonizing President Chavez for his forthright defense of Palestinian rights and condemnation of Israel's crimes against humanity during its blitz of Gaza.[71] For these acts of courage the 51 US Jewish organizations branded Chavez an "anti-Semitic", even going so far as to accuse him of fomenting an *assault* on a Jewish community center in Caracas. When the arsonists were arrested, the *assault* was revealed to have been carried out by center employees hired by the local Jewish notables.[72]

Global Zionism has targeted Argentina and Brazil. Argentinean Jews have a history of ambiguous feelings toward the state of Israel and Zionism. Early twentieth century Jews established farming and cattle ranches—the legendary "Jewish Gauchos"— while urban artisans and working class Jews were active in socialist, anarchist, communist and left wing Yiddish organizations. The mid-century generation (1940-60) of professionals, businesspeople, academics and bankers divided between leftist anti-Zionists and Zionists. Both suffered attacks from the pro-fascist sectors of the dominant mass-based populist Peronist regime. The 1960s to 1970s saw a profound generational split—characteristic of all Argentinean society—especially under the military dictatorships of (1966-1973) and (1976-1982). A significant contingent of university-based students and professors, psychologists and professionals of Jewish ancestry joined urban guerrillas and radical mass movements and suffered a "*disproportionate*" number of deaths by torture and 'disappearances'. During the worst years of terror, the Israeli government retained relations with the bloodiest of the military regimes (Videla, 1976), overlooking its anti-Semitic proclivities in order to trade in arms and military technologies. At the same time, Israel promoted Jewish immigration to Israel, securing passage of Zionist and non-Zionist Jews to Israel.

The decimation of the generation of young non-Zionist Argentine revolutionaries of Jewish ancestry and the subsequent post-dictatorial neo-liberal electoral regimes, saw the rise of new groups of wealthy Argentine Zionist Jews who grew to dominate local community organizations. They deepened ties with Israel and more recently established extensive links with the US ZPC. Once again, however, under the pro-Israel Menem regime (1980-90) anti-Semitic terrorists bombed a major Jewish civic center killing and maiming scores of Jews in downtown Buenos Aires. Investigations of police complicity were aborted by the Menem regime. Israel 'overlooked' Menem's "negligence" and instead exploited Jewish fear to offer extremely favorable terms for Argentine Jews to immigrate (including paid travel, subsidized housing in the occupied territories—education, jobs etc.).[73] The decline of leftwing activity during the 1980s and 1990s was accompanied by the de-radicalization of secular Jewish offspring, especially in the professional classes. With de-industrialization, Jews, who had formed the backbone of the previous progressive national bourgeoisie, turned to emigration, finance, real estate and Zionism.[74] The severe depression and financial crash of 2001-2002 led to the mass impoverishment of all Argentines (poverty levels hit 50% in December 2001-2002) including otherwise prosperous middle class Jews.[75] They joined the popular mass neighborhood assemblies calling for the return of their savings, the end of neo-liberal policies and politicians and the restoration of their jobs.

The subsequent economic recovery and commodity boom (2003-2008) led to a sharp de-radicalization and the ascendance of Jewish Zionist bankers, real estate and media moguls as the principal leaders in the Argentine community. Their influential role in business and the center-left Kirchner regime led to a shift toward closer relations with the ZPC – including increased efforts to include Israel as a member of the regional integration treaty MERCOSUR.[76] From the US side, the ZPC—especially the ADL and AIPAC, through their servile Secretary of State Clinton and US Congressional clients, fabricated an Islamic Iranian terrorist conspiracy in Latin America, especially in the region of the Argentine-Brazilian-Paraguayan frontier. On October 27, 2009, Zionist Congressman Elliot Engle, head of the Subcommittee on Western Hemispheric Affairs of the Foreign Relations Committee, opened hearings focusing on "Iran's expanding influence in Latin America", calling new trade ties between Iran and Brazil "a threat to the region and the security of the US".[77]

Faced with the leftist regimes in Venezuela, Bolivia and Ecuador opposed to US and Israeli colonial wars and with Brazil and Argentina's public opposing Israel's crimes in Gaza, Israel launched its US and Latin American agents on a propaganda blitz to counter the overwhelming public rejection of Israeli policies. President Shamir followed a disastrous failed tour by thuggish Zio-fascist Foreign Minister Lieberman, gaining trade and investment concessions in Brazil and Argentina.[78] Shamir's visit benefited especially through the contacts and leverage of local millionaire and billionaire Zionist business leaders. Nevertheless, Brazil, which has major trade and investment ties especially in gas and oil with Iran, has no intention of pandering to Israel.[79] In Argentina, the Zionist connection continues to limit any major openings to the Arab-Iranian investments.

Overall, the Zionist offensive and expanding local power base has resulted in mixed results: a major outflow of supporters in Venezuela and diminished influence in Bolivia and Ecuador. In contrast, Zionists have increased their influence in Brazil and Argentina.

The enormous growth of Israeli power in Europe and the US, and the new Zionist offensive in Latin America is part of the "globalization" of Zionism. But the process is not linear. An especially *hard sell* for overseas Zionists are the repeated horrendous massacres by Israeli military forces, the blatant dispossession of Palestinians and the aggressive militarism pushed by the ZPC and Israel in the Middle East and South Asia. As a result, public hostility is growing worldwide; and there is a profound disconnect between the 80% to 90% of Israeli Jews who defend Gaza war crimes and land seizures and the rest of the world.[80] This is evidenced by the United Nations General Assembly vote on the *Goldstone Report*, which was endorsed by an almost ten to one margin. Moreover, in the case of the leftist regimes in Latin America, there is a significant reversal of Zionist influence. There are equally important cracks in the Zionist monolith among North American Jews and former Zionist fellow travelers. The continued "failure of nerve" or "intellectual treason"[81] of the American left academics and their "Marxist" journals to even discuss the role of the ZPC in making war policy has not stopped a breakthrough of Zionist critics, even in some mass media outlets.

Jewish-Zionist Cultural-Political Hegemony in the US

Jewish Zionist hegemony over the political narrative in the US has grown in recent years, evidenced by the support or, at most, tepid criticism, found in the major literary and political journals and magazines.[82] In the beginning the ZPC imposed their view that Israeli conquest and wars against the native people of Palestine and its Muslim neighbors was a war of "national liberation" or "independence". This first phase culminated with Jewish-Zionist success in convincing President Johnson to cover up Israel's bombing of the USS *Liberty* during the Six Day War.[83] From the 1970-90s Zionist-Jewish hegemony extended from its traditional bastion in the film, TV and radio mass media to a whole series of former left-of-center and conservative weekly and monthly publications and the establishment of new publications on the far right.[84] The formerly liberal *New Republic* became a pulpit for virulent attacks on any critics of Israel.[85] *Commentary*, formerly a liberal cultural journal, became a mouthpiece for neo-conservative apologists of Israeli wars … and war crimes … The conservative *National Review* moved firmly into the 'Israel First' camp, purging any critical dissent on Israel and its unconditional supporters in the US. As Zionist hegemony in intellectual and popular cultural print and mass media was established, committed Israel-Firsters gained influential positions in US State Department and foreign policy apparatus.[86] "Think Tanks", thinly veiled propaganda mills, produced pro-Israel position papers.[87] Their staff elbowed their way into the mass media as "experts" and into foreign policy advisory positions serving various politicians and Administrations. They rose to the highest levels of government in the Clinton Administration and expanded further during the Bush-Obama regimes.[88] Zionist entry into key positions of structural political power mirrored their long march through the cultural institutions. Their influence was reinforced by billionaire Jewish-Zionists' contributions to established think tanks, like the Brookings Institute, and to both political parties. Contributions influenced the nominations and candidates for office from local mayors to the Presidency of the United States.

It is estimated that as high as 60% of Democratic Party contributions came from *Israel First* benefactors, securing an automatic 90% Congressional vote on whatever issue the Israeli Foreign Office marks as priority for its US Fifth Column.[89] With very rare exceptions neither liberal, progressive, radical or "Marxist" writers, academics, editors, journalists broach the issue of Zionist-Jewish cultural-political hegemony, nor its economic structural underpinnings.[90] The "left" is equally hegemonized by Zionist-Jewish influence, to the point that not a few join the vile ad hominem chorus slandering critics of the ZPC as "veering on anti-Semitism"...[91]

Even today, at the end of the first year of the Obama regime, the Zionist presence in strategic positions in foreign policy making has been ignored by leftist and liberal critics of US Middle East policy. Few, if any critics, look at the *structural* determinants of that policy. One is more likely to find "data" in the business press. For example, an article in the *Financial Times,* criticizing President Obama and Secretary of State Hillary Clinton's "inconsistent" position on Israeli settlements in Palestine's West Bank, points out that "...problems with the administrations message—including its inconsistent policy on Israel-Palestine—can be traced back to the White House, where Chief of Staff Rahm Emanuel (dual Israeli-US citizen) keeps a firm grip on foreign policy. Some ex-diplomats say they have never seen power so centralized ... Mrs. Clinton's own deputy, Jim Steinberg, is widely perceived as a White House enforcer, who polices even relatively minor policy statements that often leaves State Department spokesmen [sic] mouthing near meaningless talking points."[92] Emanuel has been active in the Israeli military and is suspected of ties to its spy agency (MOSSAD). Steinberg is just a high powered "native born" Israel Firster, marginalizing the State Department from any alternative policies to pandering to Israel and its US Fifth Column.

Hegemonized American liberals and leftists maintain their "support" for Israel on the basis of the fiction that the "bad" Israelis are the fanatical *Likud* party leaders while Labor and Kadima party leaders and the Israeli people want peace and a just settlement. Unfortunately for these supporters of "progressive" Zionism, Defense Minister Ehud Barak ,who directed the bloody massacre in Gaza, is the leader of the Labor Party and is backed by his party in support of all the new aggressive Israeli land seizures and colonial settlements. The genocidal wars and violent settlements have the support of the vast majority of the Israeli Jewish population. Public opinion polls carried out by the Israel National News published in mid-November 2009 reveal that 53.2% of Israeli's say the solution to the conflict with the Palestinian people is their forceful dispossession and ethnic cleansing—"transfer" is the Zionist euphemism for a crime against humanity.[93] Such are the "just wars" receiving unconditional support by the '51' Presidents of the Major American Jewish Organizations.

The point is that not even the Israeli-Jewish majority's embrace of a totalitarian final solution shakes Zionist hegemony in the US. The embrace of inconvenient positions, such as genocide approval, is not publicized in the Zionist mass media. Instead we continue to hear the chattering classes mouthing the clichés of a "dialogue" and "negotiated solution" between the expropriators and the dispossessed.

The question of Zionist cultural and political hegemony, to the extent that it is even acknowledged by non-Jews and Jews, revolves around several mistaken partially distorted conceptions. One key idea held by anti-Semites and Zionists alike is that Jews possess special qualities ("blood" or "genetic"). Many cite the importance of a Jewish historical tradition, which emphasizes education and learning—as if such traditions were not found in other cultures. Others still, claim success and power comes from knowledge, merit and achievement. Recent studies refute the idea of a special, unique Jewish "gene pool"—as most contemporary Askanazi Jews are descendants of Central Asian Khazari converts to Judaism in the 8th Century A.D., who subsequently were pushed into Eastern Europe by the Mongols and beyond.[94] Israelis are not descendants of the ancient Jews of Israel, many of whom converted to Christianity and later Islam and whose descendants are most certainly the modern-day Palestinians (as conceded by early Zionists myth-makers, like David Ben-Gurion).

Secondly, for over one thousand years, Jewish "scholarship" revolved around sterile debates and exegeses of the minutiae of the Talmud and bodies of law based on religious myths. Critical philosophers like Spinoza were regarded as renegades. The rise of scholarship and scientific thinking among Jews coincided with the growth of the Enlightenment and the establishment of liberal laws, which opened doors permitting promising Jewish scholars and scientists to break out of the sterile confines of the Rabbinal intellectual ghettos. Many of the great thinkers were called "Jews" because of their ancestry, like Spinoza, Karl Marx and Leon Trotsky although they did not practice Judaism nor identify as "Jews". The recognition and success of Jews came from business and financial activity as well as from occupations like money managers in the West and overseers of feudal lords in Poland.[95] A Jewish-authored scholarly history of the Jewish people was not written until the 19th century and even then, it treated biblical legends as fact.[96]

Equally questionable is the notion that the rise of Jewish-Zionist hegemony is a product of "merit" or "achievement". But here we must distinguish between the masses of Jews who occupy middle or lower middle class positions in society and those few individuals who have made major contributions. Moreover it is important to not confuse the rise of individuals to economic power through the exploitation of labor, the extraction of rent from tenants and speculation, and that achievement attributable to "merit", to skills applied to advancing knowledge for the greater good of humanity. Zionists' "superior race" theorists lump successful Wall Street speculators with innovative scholars as examples of "Jewish superiority", purportedly justifying or "explaining" hegemony. The corpus of Zionist race theories, which claim a homogenous 'Jewish' people bound by common history and horizontal and vertical ties, is more an ideological manifesto ignoring profound class and even ideological divisions (at least in the past and perhaps emerging today).

Jewish-Zionist hegemony in the US is the result of a supra- or meta-historical mythology with mystical religious foundations in the Old Testament. The rise of American Zionism is tied to a virulent exclusivist tribal religious loyalty to Israel as the "mother state". The driving force of US Zionism is the *subordination* of US civil society organizations and the instrumentalization of the US military and economic resources to service Israeli colonial expansion and projections of power in the Middle East.

What needs to be understood is that the present subjection of US Middle East policy to the Zionist Power Configuration is a result of the latter's accumulation of power and of political-cultural conditions within the US, which weakened the articulation of alternative values and policies and a defense of American working class interests embodied in a democratic foreign policy.

The Decline of US National Identity and Working Class Politics

The rise of Zionism, as a virulent form of tribal-religious identity linked to a foreign state and its successful exercise of *hegemony* within US society, has been facilitated by the abdication by the US ruling class 'establishment' of any 'national' identity and its *interlocking* economic ties with Zionist power brokers in strategic economic sectors.

The "globalization" of US capitalism, the process of worldwide empire building, has shifted the focus of the US ruling class toward *international* issues as the center of its concerns, even as it intervenes in domestic economic policies to secure state protection, subsidies and bailouts, none of which trespass on Zionist priorities. Going "global" and the emergence of "global consciousness" has worked against challenging the Zionist pursuit of the colonial agenda of the state of Israel. The ZPC has filled a 'power vacuum' left by the 'globalized elite' and has been able to instill and impose a *Zionist conception* of US "national interest" that has been relatively uncontested.

The rise of the Zionist business elites into the top echelon of investment banking, financial institutions, real estate and insurance led to the inter-mixing of Zionist and non-Zionist members of the ruling class, in which one side had a deep and abiding political commitment to Israel, while the other sector gave exclusive primacy to the accumulation of wealth and guaranteeing that state economic policy ensured profits, a deregulated financial sector and bank bailouts, policies which they shared with their Zionist partners. Given the low salience of Israeli politics, the non-Zionist sectors of the ruling class were not willing or able to engage in a fight with their Zionist financial colleagues.[97]

However, there are divisions, both in government and within policy advisory bodies, over Zionist control. As mentioned earlier, the 16 major intelligence agencies issued a report on Iran's nuclear program in late 2007, which debunked the Israeli-Zionist claims of an active Iranian nuclear *weapons* program. Likewise a Pew Foundation Study of the Council on Foreign Relations, taken between October 2-November 16, 2009, found that over two-thirds of its members (67 percent) believe the US favored Israel too much—yet the same percentages claimed Obama is "striking the right balance" and "Iran is a major threat to US interest".[98] What is striking about these 'dissident' opinions within the policy elite is that they have had no impact on Obama's subservience to Israel on all major issues promoted by the ZPC. Whatever the CFR "really thinks" has not "really" affected the power of the ZPC to shape policy via its stooges in Congress and its assets in State (Clinton) and Treasury (Stuart Levey). In other words, Zionist power at the top is uncontested and free to work the lower echelons of the political system and class structure for its own interest. This includes the wholesale purchase of political parties and the retail buyout of congressional politicians on key foreign policy committees. The latter is facilitated by the success of the Israel First political action committees (PACs) which promote the selection of Zionist Congress people to key committee posts. Four of the top fifteen Congress people funded by Wall Street speculators are Zionists. Eleven of the top fifteen are Democrats, who receive 60% of their contributions from Zionist multi-millionaires in Los Angeles, New York, and south Florida and other metropolitan centers.[99]

The *political class*, party leaders, executive and congress people, have also eschewed pro-American working class economic policies, endogenous growth and the avoidance of foreign entanglements (interventionism). The political class—particularly its dominant sector—favors military driven empire building—undermining any popular democratic definition of 'national interest'. Moreover, the military nature of empire building *resonates* with the Zionist-Israeli projection of regional military power and hegemony. Military-driven imperialism weakens any effort to develop alternative US overseas economic interests and policies, especially with Muslim and Middle East oil countries, to counter Israeli-Zionist policies designed to privilege Israeli military expansion and colonial interests.

If the majority of the US ruling class has surrendered to the Zionist definitions of US Middle East policy, and facilitated the rise of Zionist hegemony, the decline of the values embedded in working class solidarity and defense of republican virtues and interests has opened the door for the minority of Zionist cadres to influence mass culture and civil society organizations and divert American trade union pension funds to Israeli investments with no opposition. For decades, predominantly Afro-American and Hispanic female workers in garments, textiles and related activities have been members of trade unions run by Zionist functionaries, who channeled hundreds of millions of member pension funds and dues into purchasing Israel bonds, rather than building co-operative housing as was done previously when the union workers were mostly Jews. Many current (minority) leaders of trade unions and Afro-Hispanic ethnic organizations have been co-opted by the ZPC though junkets to Israel and propaganda campaigns promoting Israeli interests. In universities, municipal politics, and professional associations, *Israel Firsters* operate to stifle any debate, let alone criticism, of Israeli war crimes. Zionists in America are the most pernicious force eliminating debate on American democratic foreign policy options in the Middle East and favoring unconditional submission to Israel. Millions of individuals, who may question the "*Israel First*" option, are frightened, intimidated and/or unwilling to face the onslaught of organized, zealous Zionist-Jewish notables, who can and will influence their employers and jeopardize their jobs and promotions.

Conclusion: Alternatives to Zionist Hegemony

In other countries, especially where independent class-conscious trade unions, autonomous and organized anti-Zionist professional and academic groups exist, Zionist power in civil society is contested, challenged and its heinous blackballing of critics is weakened. Where internationalist movements are strong, as in support for Palestinian resistance to Israeli colonialism, the local ZPC has not been able to use their economic power and media ownership to impose their hegemony over civil society. This is especially true in those locales where the international solidarity movement is active in impacting society.

While there are pockets of international solidarity among some universities and trade unions in the US, especially the dock and warehouse workers in San Francisco, the major potential counterweight to Zionist Israel First hegemony in the US would be in a revival of *patriotic working class consciousness*. America's "special relation" with Israel has been at an enormous cost to the working class, amounting to over $1.5 trillion dollars in foreign aid, loan guarantees, hijacked technological innovations, lost overseas investment opportunities, not to mention the wars on Israel's behalf and the lives lost in fighting Israel's war in Iraq. There is a 'material base' for a mass patriotic working people's revolt against the crass submission of the entire political class to the ZPC and its patrons in Tel-Aviv.

But today tens of millions of Americans are disillusioned with "patriotic" appeals, whose purpose is rather to promote imperial wars (including ironically wars for Israel) at the expense of their living standards. Right wing pro-capitalist politicians use patriotic rhetoric to deflect attention from the domestic failures of capitalism and the massive transfers of wealth to Goldman Sachs and other Wall Street speculators. The devaluation of "*patriotism*" is evident in the right wing's perverse manipulation of '*nationalism*' to turn native born workers against immigrant workers, instead of against the ZPC's costly pro-Israel agenda. This, in turn, hinders the growth of a national popular movement against the Wall Street speculators at home and the wars for Israel and Empire abroad.

What is striking about the lack of mass based movements against Wall Street is the fact that literally less than 5% of the population even trusts the financial sector. A vast outpouring of letters and protests denounced Obama's initial bank bailout plan, forcing a temporary postponement. Unorganized mass resentment persists and is smoldering, waiting for effective popular organization.

Zionists in public office, in the Pentagon, executive branch and the White House, who design and promote war policies and military-driven sanctions, are in the forefront of shedding American working class lives, especially now when jobless American workers, including many minorities, are forced to seek employment in the military. However, family and relatives of the Zionist power configuration, in and out of the government, who *promote* US wars for Israel in the Middle East, are rarely to be found in the Armed Forces, least of all at the front lines (or for that matter in any war zone). If we exclude non-Zionist Jews—mostly immigrants from the former Eastern Bloc and USSR—the figure would be one-thirtieth of one percent. It is a biting irony that more American Zionists are more eager to join the Israeli 'Defense' Forces than to put on an American uniform. A class-based soldier's anti-war movement could be organized and energized under the banner: "ISRAEL DOESN'T TELL U.S. WORKERS WHO TO FIGHT" if the left and pacifists were not so captive to their Jewish *'sensibilities'*. The anti-war leaders have been reluctant to raise the issue of the Zionist/ Israeli influence in promoting US war policies, even though the possibility of war with Iran has been the most bare-faced instance of this.

Genuine patriotic solidarity is weak at the top and bottom, lacking any meaningful recall of our anti-colonial, anti-slavery, anti-imperialist and anti-fascist identity. In contrast, the *Zionist fifth column* is driven by a powerful mythological-tribal race-driven identity, which in some cases is religious driven and in others embedded in a deep-rooted secular sense of racial superiority.

Israeli hegemony, embedded in a Zion-centric cultural universe, has not been challenged by Anglo-America's flaccid intellectuals. Their intellectual cowardice is covered by a thin veneer of "cosmopolitan" impotence. Their pusillanimous silence and even complicity is intended to *'protect the sensitivities'* of their Zionist colleagues regarding any forthright critique of Zionist power in America. Only a revived working class movement, which recovers its historical memory of class solidarity and inspires the popular imagination with an independent American republic free from foreign dictates, will be able to displace Zionist hegemony and Wall Street pillage.[100]

Our study raises several central questions that need to be addressed by Americans concerned about Zionist power and hegemony over public debate regarding US wars for Israel in the Middle East.

Can we oppose Israeli war crimes and expansion and US government support of Israel by confronting the ZPC?

Can we open a debate on US Middle East policy by fighting Zionist authoritarianism, witch hunts and hate crimes?

Can we discuss and propose a democratic foreign policy, which opposes military intervention, sanctions and economic blockades, by tackling American militarists and Israel's foreign agents?

If we answer in the affirmative, what can be done?

What practical measures can be pursued and supported?

- *First and foremost, we can organize and demand a peace movement galvanized under the banner, "**No to War on Iran for Israel**"—a war which has been almost unilaterally pushed by Israel and the ZPC, with their Congressional stooges in tow[101].*
- We can educate the American public about the Obama

regime's charade of *talking* peace to the American people while *supporting* the Israeli war machine; of talking about an evenhanded Middle East policy while appointing committed Zionists to top policy positions.

- We can demand the Justice Department enforce the Foreign Agents Registration Act toward the '51 Presidents of Major American Jewish Organizations' and especially AIPAC.

- We should oppose all dual citizens' appointments to key policymaking posts.

- We should demand that Undersecretary of Treasury and *Israel Firster* Stuart Levey be investigated and prosecuted for gross malfeasance of office for his refusal to investigate the illegal billion-dollar money laundering operations by US Zionists in the funding of illegal Jewish settlements in the West Bank, and for his promotion of economic sanctions against trade with Iran, which have cost US workers thousands of jobs and the crippled US economy billions of dollars in lost trade.

- We should oppose military and economic aid to Israel, especially when the average per capita income of Israelis exceeds that of 40% of Americans.

- We should demand the end of trade privileges for Israel in light of the US' multi-billion dollars trade deficit with Israel, which has destroyed tens of thousands of American jobs in industry and services.

- We should combat widespread Zionist hate propaganda, organized and publicized by the ZPC, against Muslin Americans and Arab Americans, and their cultural foundations and charities.

- We should demystify Zionist claims that the Jews' ancestral homeland is Israel, rather than North Africa and Central Asia, and that there is no historic basis for the *Right of Return.*

- We should support the class and popular struggle against finance, real estate and insurance billionaires (Wall Street) for their pillage of the American economy and exploitation of American workers and for their corruption of American politicians to serve *their* interests and US and Israeli war aims.

Endnotes

1   The major sources which inform this article include: *The Daily Alert*, a bulletin published daily by the 51 Presidents of Major American Jewish Organizations; press releases and reports published by the American

Israel Public Affairs Committee, *The New York Times, Washington Post,* the *Wall Street Journal,* the *Financial Times,* the *Boston Globe* and the US Congressional Research Services. The mailings of articles from a plethora of publications by Sid Shniad were of enormous help, though, of course, the analysis and interpretations found in this article are solely my responsibility, Web sites such as Information Clearing House (www.informationclearinghouse.info), Al Jazeera and the BBC were also consulted on a daily basis.

2   The claim is found on the webpage of the *Daily Alert,* the official propaganda vehicle of the Conference of Presidents.

3   See the report prepared by the Jewish Community Task Force published in the *Boston Globe,* Sept. 20, 2009. See Elliott Abrams on the "threat" of intermarriages, *Faith and Fear: How Jews can Survive in Christian America,* (NY Free Press 1999). See Natan Sharansky, "Assimilation is Eating the Jews", (*Haaretz*, 11/8/09)

4   In the face of faltering interest in Israel among young Jews, the Anti-Defamation League, Bnai Brth, Chabad House and Hillel have organized all-expenses-paid summer junkets to Israel – with mixed results.

5   See Stephan Lendman, "Jews Against Zionism,: Dec. 7, 2009 at http://sjlendman.blogspot.com/2009/12/jews-against-zionism.html The list includes over a dozen secular and religious groups..

6   See Yakov Rabkin, *Jewish Opposition to Zionism* (Halifax: Fernwood 2006) for a religious critique of Israel and its overseas Zionist supporters. For a secular version see Israel Shahak *Jewish History, Jewish Religion* (London Pluto Press 2002).

7   See Barbara Yaffe "Over-the-top criticism of Israel is the new face of anti-semitism", *Vancouver Sun,* December 2, 2009. Systematic campaigns to fire critics of Israel by the '51 Presidents', especially the ADL, led to the firing of Professor Norman Finklestein and prolonged academic harassment for Professor Robinson at the University of California at Santa Barbara and Nadia Abu El-Haj at the University of Chicago/Barnard, as well as numerous other writers and academics in Middle Eastern studies programs at Columbia and UCLA. See Stephan Lendman, "Will Congress Criminalize Israel Criticism", Dec. 4, 2009, http://sjlendman.blogspot.com/2009/12/will-congress-criminalize-anti-semitism.html.

8   A handbook put by Congregation of Conservative Synagogues details the precise tactics to be used in pressuring civic and political groups and leveraging them to support the Israeli state line.

9   For a detailed account see my *The Power of Israel in the United States* (Atlanta: Clarity Press, 2006) especially Ch 1-3; *Rulers and Ruled in the US Empire* (Atlanta: Clarity Press, 2007) especially Ch 8–10; *Zionism, Militarism and the Decline of US Power* (Atlanta: Clarity Press, 2008); *Global Depression and Regional Wars* (Atlanta: Clarity Press, 2009) Ch 9–11.

10   In their otherwise fine book *The Israel Lobby and US Foreign Policy* (New York: Farrar, Straus, and Giroux, 2007), the authors John Mearsheimer and Stephen Walt confine their analyses to Washington and political pressure on the legislative branch by neo-conservative

Zionist Jews, (see Ch 4 "What is the 'Israel' Lobby", pp. 111–150). Needless to say, the entire spectrum of Zionists from the Left to Right attempted to trash the book, fabricating non-facts, ad hominem slanders and minimizing the scope and depth of the findings.

11   A survey of the *Daily Alert*, the propaganda organ of the '51', between January 2001 to December 3, 2009—namely over 2500 issues—revels nary a single critical article on any Israeli action. Even more revealing, every issue echoes the policy line of the Israeli government, defends every Israeli massacre, military invasion and dispossession of Palestinians, and condemns every human rights group, country, and political leader that criticizes Israel in the best fashion of the hardest line unconditional Stalinist apologist of the Soviet purge trials of the 1930s.

12   Pluralist political theorists emphasize the importance of numerical weight of the working class electorate as a counterweight to the great concentrations of wealth, property and media power of the capitalist class under the misconception that unorganized masses are an equal power to an organized financial oligarchy. The classic formulation of pluralist theory is found in Robert Dahl, *Who Governs* (New Haven: Yale University Press, 1961).

13   Between the publication of the *Goldstone Report* in the fall of 2009 and the end of November, the *Daily Alert* published an average of three articles a day defending Israel war crimes, viciously attacking the *Report*, and slandering the author, Richard Goldstone, drawing on articles from the *Washington Post*, the *Wall Street Journal*, *The New York Times*, *The Jerusalem Post* and the entire stable of Israel-First "experts" housed in the Zionist think tanks. Once Netanyahu established trashing the *Goldstone Report* as a 'number-one' priority, the entire international Zionist propaganda network went into full gear, especially in North America. The *Daily Alert* published over 30 articles savaging the 'Report'. Its affiliates went into overdrive securing over 80% of Congressional support demanding that President Obama reject the Report and veto its approval by the Security Council. Netanyahu and his American agents succeeded—overfilling their quota of articles published in all the US mass media and securing submissive Congressional votes. See also Paul Craig Roberts "Israel Lobby Routs Obama", Information Clearing House (www.informationclearinghouse. info) November 12, 2009.

14   According to Aljazeera.Net, November 4, 2009, Steven Rothman, a prominent Zionist Democratic congressman from New Jersey, claimed to have read only the 20 page executive s*ummary* of the *Report*, prepared by the office of his fellow-Zionist Congressman Berman (D-California), instead of the full 575 page report—a *summary* full of errors, lies and distortions, which were pointed out by Justice Goldstone.

15   See Thalif Deen "U.N. Affirms Israel-Hamas War Crimes Report" *Inter Press News Service,* (www.informationclearinghouse.info) November 6, 2009.

16   Jewish anti-Zionist organizations in North America, including Independent Jewish Voices, have played an important role in building the

Boycott Disinvestment and Sanctions (BDS) movement against Israeli war crimes: See their web site at http://bdsmovement.net. Also see http://www.independentjewishvoices.ca

17   For articles and reports on the BDS among trade unions, see independentjewishvoices.ca

18   Trials on Israeli war criminals are scheduled in Belgium, Spain and possibly the UK.

19   Among the publications we can include *The Nation, The Progressive* and *Mother Jones* as well as most of the Marxist quarterlies,

20   The Zionist *fifth column* and their apologists claim that analysts, academic researches and journalists who document the power of Israel in the US, are reminiscent of past "anti-Semitic conspiracy theorists writing about secret Jewish cabals". This slander of empirical researchers overlooks the fact that most studies rely on public documents, including boasts by the Zionist organizations themselves, as well as the testimony of ex-functionaries of AIPAC. This slander is part of the campaign led by the "anti" Defamation League; Abe Foxman, to intimidate and discredit serious research.

21   *Haaretz* 11/10/09.

22   ibid.

23   ibid.

24   Shlomo Sand *The Invention of the Jewish People* (London: Verso 2009) Ch 3 and 4. Arthur Koestler *The Thirteenth Tribe: The Khazan Empire and its Heritage* (New York: Random House 1976).

25   The annual AIPAC meetings, attended by the vast majority of US Congressmen and executive officials, sponsor the participation Israel's top officials, who literally dictate top Israeli priorities to be implemented by the Zionist delegates and their congressional flunkies in the audience.

26   See Grant Smith, "Foreign Agents", Institute for Research: Middle East Policy (IRMEP), Washington , 2008 at http://www.irmep.org.

27   From the early 1950s to the mid 1960s, the US Justice Department (especially under Robert Kennedy) sought to have the forerunner of AIPAC (American Zionist Council) register as a foreign agent. Influential Zionists undermined his efforts. See Grant Smith, *America's Defense Line: The Justice Department's Battle to Register the Israel Lobby as Agents of a Foreign Power*, (Washington: Institute for Research: Middle Eastern Policy, 2008).

28   See my *The Power of Israel in the United States* (2006) cc 5-8; Lenni Brenner *Jews in America Today* (New Jersey: Lyle Stuart 1986); Ch 3 Lee O'Brien *American Jewish Organizations and Israel* (Washington D.C: Institute for Palestinian Studies 1986).

29   Declassified documents of the US Justice Dept. revealing the role of the major Zionist organization (American Zionist Council) as Israeli foreign agents can be found in Grant Smith, *Declassified Deceptions* (Washington: IRMEP 2007) pp183 -200. Grant Smith, *Foreign Agents: The American Israel Public Affairs Committee from the 1963 Fulbright Hearings to the 2005 Espionage Scandal,* (IRMEP, Washington D.C., 2007) Ch. 1.

30   Grant Smith *Spy Trade: How Israel's Lobby Undermines America's Economy* (1RMEP: Washington D.C. 2009) See pp 66 passion

"Military Industrial Espionage" and pp 120-138 for unclassified FBI documentation.

31   *Forward,* December 23, 2005.

32   For a complete inventory of Kadish's theft of strategic weapons secrets see Grant Smith *Spy Trade,* pp 80, 85, 115.

33   See Grant Smith *Spy Trade,* pp 19, 43, 46, 60, 66, 67, 69, 74, 80, 122, 154.

34   *Boston Globe* 10/20/09.

35   See Ostrovsky, *By Way of Deception* (New York: St Martin's Press 1990), pp 86-88.

36   See "Carl Cameron Investigates" (Part 1-4) Fox New Network, December 17, 2001, available at http://www.informationclearinghouse.info/article5133.htm

37   James Petras, *Zionism, Militarism and the Decline of US Power* (Clarity Press: Atlanta 2008) p 156.

38   The *Washington Post, The New York Times,* and a coalition of 125 rabbis attacked the AIPAC, Rosen-Weissman spy trial as "anti-Semitic" while Amy Goodman and liberal-left pundits charged it was a violation of the First Amendment. See Grant Smith *Spy Trade* pp 117-119. Grant Smith *Foreign Agents,* pp 134-145.

39   Petras, *Zionism, Militarism and Decline of US Power,* p 156.

40   See Grant Smith *Declassified Deceptions,* p 229.

41   James Petras "Barack Obama: America's First Jewish President" Information Clearinghouse, January 31, 2008.

42   James Petras, *Global Depression and Regional Wars* (Atlanta: Clarity Press 2009) Ch 10, pp 153-155. Jewish Telegraph Agency, April 27, 2009.

43   Colonel Karen Kwiatkowski, a middle level official in the Pentagon eventually resigned in protest.

44   ibid.

45   Between November 2007 and January 2008, *The Daily Alert,* propaganda mouthpiece of the '51' Zionist organizations, reproduced over two dozen articles from the major media condemning the November 2007 US National Intelligence Estimate and parroting Israeli disinformation on Iranian nuclear bomb.

46   Mearsheimer and Walt *The Israel Lobby ,* Ch 6, Dominating Public Discourse, pp 168-196; Lee O'Brien *American Jewish Organizations and Israel* (Washington, DC: Institute for Palestine Studies, 1986) Ch 5.

47   Despite the general consensus among most Washington observers and congressional staff people regarding the power of what they call the *Israel Lobby* and despite the enormous influence of known Zionists in important foreign policy positions over the past 20 years (in the Clinton, Bush and Obama regimes) one looks in vain for any critical essays on Zionist power in the *New Left Review, New Politics, Against the Current, Socialist Register, International Socialist Review, Critique,* etc. If anything, when a book appears, like Mearsheimer and Walt's *The Israel Lobby* or my *The Power of Israel in the US,* we are much more likely to receive a more balanced review in libertarian conservative publications like antiwar.com and informationclearinghouse.

info, than from what appear to be Marxist...Zionist fellow travelers. Exceptional cases of critiques of Zionist power have appeared in *Canadian Dimension* and *Z Magazine*, though I am told that "*left*" Zionists readers have complained and threatened to cancel subscriptions and/ or contributions.

48   See Alex Cockburn and Jeffrey St. Clair, *The Politics of Anti-Semitism* (Oakland: AK Press 2003).

49   Mearsheimer and Walt, *The Israel Lobby, op cit.*

50   Several publications have enumerated the media outlets, which parrot the political line of the ZPC and the Israeli regime, principally the *Wall Street Journal*, the *Washington Post* (and with occasional minor deviations) *The New York Times*, the *Chicago Tribune*, *The New York Post*, *The Sun*, as well as CNN, CBS, NBS and, of course, Murdoch's Fox News. However, these studies lack a systematic analysis of the organizational links between the pro-Zionist/Israel message, the media owners, editors and directors and their ties to the ZPC. Glimpses of the Zionist Power Configuration in the media appear in the writings of Edward Herman, Norman Finklestein, Grant Smith, Alexander Cockburn, Joel Kovel, Mearsheimer and Walt. A general resume is found in Edward Abboud, *Invisible Enemy*, (Virginia: Vox 2003) Ch 4, 49.

51   Most of the essays that identified Zionist zealots in power positions in the Bush regime have been published by the website, antiwar. com. The authors include Justin Raimundo, Philip Giraldi, Paul Craig Roberts, Alison Weir and Jonathan Cook.

52   Exceptions include Edward Said's writings, Edward Tivnan, *The Lobby*, Grant Smith, *Spy Trade*. See also Edward Said and Christopher Hitchens editors, *Blaming the Victim* (London: Verso 1988).

53   Privileging "Jewish" or "Israeli" sources is the favorite device of writers across the political spectrum and includes non-Jews and Jewish critics in all the progressive blogs and published work.

54   This is an argument that I have heard and read from some of the leaders of newly formed Jewish organizations critical of Israel. One wonders whether this is not a replay of the exclusivist outlook featured in the rabbinical canon: keeping the 'dirty wash' in the family.

55   See Stephen Lendman, "Jews Against Zionism", December 7, 2009 at http://sjlendman.blogspot.com.

56   The major trade unions supporting the Boycott, Divestment and Sanctions Movement include Canadian public sector unions, Irish trade union confederation, British, Italian, French, Greek and Spanish trade unions.

57   In recent times the most notorious effort by the US and Canadian ZPC to blackball and oust academic critics of Israel revolved around the tenure case of Norman Finklestein at DePaul University and the censure of William Robinson at UC Santa Barbara. The ZPC succeeded in securing the ouster of Finklestein despite strong faculty support and several major book publications but failed in the Robinson case. In Canada the ZPC has set up a nationwide campaign to ban activities around the anti-apartheid issue on university campuses.

58   *Daily Alert* has re-published over two dozen op-ed pieces from in the

Washington Post, Wall Street Journal and Zionist think-tanks in Washington defending Israeli violations of international law from November 1 to December 7, 2009.

59   The scorecard is pro-Israel articles 49 to 1 article critical between October-November 2009.

60   From September 1 to December 1, none of the above mentioned media allowed a single critical non-Zionist commentator to present a favorable view of the *Goldstone Report.*

61   Ultra-Zionist academics holed up in so called prestigious Ivy league universities include Michael Walzer at Princeton, and Dershowitz at Harvard, Friedman at University of London, Kagan at Yale, Cohen at Johns Hopkins and a flock of others penning apologies for Israeli state terror.

62   See the excerpts in the *Daily Alert* from September through December 2009.

63   Michael Walzer, *Just Wars and Unjust Wars* (New York: Basic Books 2006. President Obama's address to the Nobel Peace Prize committee in December 2009 relied heavily on Walzer's "Just War" polemic

64   When Goldstone forwarded his reply to Congressman Berman detailing the lies and distortions in the latter's 'summary', which accompanied a US Congressional resolution defending Israeli war crimes, Berman merely repeated his fabrications. Such are our contemporary "Stalinists" who know only one "truth"—how to parrot and defend the Israeli party line. What is amusing is how few of the lifelong Jewish anti-Stalinist writers have raised any questions about the neo-Stalinist Zionists in their midst....

65   The combination of scientist, racist and ideologue among Zionist advocates of the biblical myths is not uncommon among twentieth century colonial and imperial regimes. On Israeli-Zionist fabricated racial myths see Nadia Abu El-Haj, *Facts on the Ground* op cit; Joel Zerulavel, *Recovered Roots* (Chicago: University of Chicago Press 1995) Ch2, 3; Israel Shahak *Jewish History, Jewish Religion* (London: Pluto Press 1994) Ch 2 -4.

66   Theodore Adorno et al, *The Authoritarian Personality* (New York: Basic Books 1950). It is curious that very few psychological-clinical studies of Zionist socio-pathological behavior have been produced. Jewish psychologists and sociologists, many of whom claim expertise in the 'psychology of terrorism' and the effects of fear on civilian populations, are especially prominent in their embrace of Israeli crimes against humanity. Given the large number of Jewish psychiatrists and psychologists, this suggests how important ideology is in defining scientific projects.

67   According to the *Guardian* (November 16, 2009), 50% of MP's in the shadow cabinet are Conservative Friends of Israel who have received ten million pounds over the past 8 years. The British television Channel 4 documentary program *Dispatches* broadcast 'Inside the Pro-Israel Lobby' with investigative journalist Peter Osborne, from November 16-20, 2009. This astonishing report revealed the deep penetration of the three major parties by the Zionist Power Configuration and the centrality of lobby funding in securing British defense of Israeli poli-

cies and war crimes. Zionist control of the British mass media is as pervasive as in the US: the International Television (ITV) network's two most influential companies, Carlton Communications and Granada Media Plc, are under Zionist management and ownership. The BBC TV has turned from being a fairly objective news outlet to being a cheap propagandist over the past half decade, under the direction of managing director Tony Cohen. Zionist ownership of the principal dailies include *The Daily Express*, the *Daily Star* and the Murdoch chain (*The Sun, The Times, The News of the World*) which controls over 80% of British readership.

68   Channel 4, *op cit.*

69   See the web site <http://www.independentjewishvoices.ca> for complete coverage of the Canadian government's close ties with the leading Zionist organizations, its pursuit of Israel's agenda and moves to *criminalize criticism* of Israel. See also the news report on the Canadian Jewish Congress *Vancouver Sun*, Dec. 2, 2009.

70   *The New York Times,* November 11, 2009.

71   See Eric Wingerter and Justin Delacour, "Playing the Anti-Semitism Card against Venezuela" http://www.venezuelanalysis.com, Sept. 4, 2009.

72   ibid.

73   Interviews with Argentine Jewish immigrants to Israel, April-May 2004, March 2006.

74   The Argentine Communist Party was said to have a greater representation of members in the financial sector than any other party in the world. Its Jewish members were more likely from the Co-operative Banks than the meat packing or car manufacturing sector .Interviews, March 2006.

75   Interviews Buenos Aires, April–May 2002.

76   President Cristina Fernandez met with President Shamir and Abe Foxman of the ADL in Buenos Aires and with the top Zionist leaders during a visit to New York, before and after speaking at the United Nations. Fernandez is the leading proponent of Israel's privileged status in MERCOSUR.

77   Engel's threats had little impact: Brazil signed over 20 trade and investment agreements with Iran and Lula dismissed US Zionist efforts to dictate foreign policy to the dustbin of history. On December 4, 2009, Secretary of State Clinton threatened dire consequences for countries developing economic ties with Iran, targeting Brazil, Bolivia and Venezuela (*La Jornada,* December 4, 2009). President Evo Morales of Bolivia charged the US has no authority to speak against terrorism since it is the biggest practioner (*La Jornada*, December 13, 2009).

78   Avi Lieberman's visit was an Israeli foreign policy disaster, provoking major protests in Argentina and Brazil, as well as a very cold reception from heads of state.

79   Most heads of state, especially the new center-left regimes governing most of the region, have unpleasant memories of Israel's close ties with the bloody dictatorships of the 1970s and 1980s. Israel provided intelligence, military advisers and arms to the genocidal Somoza

regime in Nicaragua, Rios Mont terror state in Guatemala and the death squad regime in El Salvador. Israel had a special relation with Argentina following the bloody military coup in 1976, replacing the US as the main military supplier, overlooking the murderous campaign against all Argentine progressives including many Jews, who were taunted by anti-Semitic torturers. Bishara Bahbah, *Israel and Latin America* (New York: St. Martin's Press 1986) Ch 3, 4 5.

80   The Israeli-Jewish media, with the rare exception of an occasional article in *Ha'aretz*, was vehement in support of the rape of Gaza, as was the Israeli-Jewish public reported in a number of polls published in January 2009. Dozens of Israeli *democratic* stalwarts took beach chairs, picnic baskets and binoculars to survey the terror bombing of Gaza from adjoining hills.

81   Julian Benda, *The Betrayal of the Intellectuals*, (Boston: Beacon Press 1955).

82   Under moderate pro-Israelite editors, *The New Yorker*, the *New York Review of Books*, *The Nation* and *The Progressive* have "debated" the pro and con of Obama's pro-Israel policies avoiding any mention of the Zionist penetration of its Mid-East policy apparatus.

83   See Stephan Green *Taking Sides* (New York: Morrow 1984) Ch. 9. James Bamford, *Body of Secrets* (New York: Doubleday 2001). James Ennes, *Assault on the Liberty* (New York: Random House 1980).

84   These include the *National Review* and the *Daily Standard* on the right, the *New Republic* on the liberal left, and *The New Yorker* which publishes Seymour Hersh's exposes and hack jobs on the critics of the Zionist power structure._

85   The transformation of Jewish liberalism into virulent Zionist extremism is evident subsequent to the take-over of the *New Republic* by Martin Peretz in 1974 and Norman Podhoretz "right turn" at *Commentary* in the early 1960's. The Six Day War and Israel's military victory was a major factor in bringing out all the chauvinist strains latent within many formerly liberal and progressive Jews who subsequently combined liberal domestic politics with blind support for the most extremist measures adopted by the Jewish state.

86   Under Bush see my T*he Power of Israel in the United States*, Ch1, 2 and under Obama see my *Global Depression and Regional Wars*, Ch 9, pp 131-135 and pp 151-158.

87   See Mearscheimer and Walt, *The Israel Lobby* Ch 6, esp. 175-178. At least eleven "think tanks" function directly under Zionist control in the greater Washington/NYC area.

88   See Grant Smith, *Spy Trade*, pp. 111 – 113; *The Power of Israel in the United States*, Ch.2. Prominent Zionists in top policy positions making Middle East policy under Clinton included Dennis Ross, Martin Indyk, Richard Holbrook, Lawrence Summers, Robert Rubin, Madeline Albright, Eliot Cohen and a host of other political advisers.

89   See Mearscheimer and Walt, *Israel Lobby,* pp. 153-62, 163-64.

90   Among the leading left academics ignoring ZPC influence in the lead-up to the Iraqi war and Iranian sanctions include Perry Anderson, Robert Brenner, Noam Chomsky, Howard Zinn, among a long list of who's who in the Anglo-American left.

91   One prominent progressive rabbi suggested to me that my critique of the ZPC was "veering on Anti-Semitism"; others have even raised the idea that identifying organized Zionist influence over US Middle East policy "reads like the Protocols of Zion". See Norman Finkelstein on the abuse of the anti-Semitic "blood libel" (to quote Israel's prime minister) in *The Holocaust Industry*, Verso 2003, especially Ch. 3, and Joel Kovel, *Overcoming Zionism*, Ann Arbor Pluto Press, 2007, Ch 1-3.

92   *Financial Times* November 21/22, 2009, p.2.

93   Information Clearing House, November 20, 2009.

94   Shlomo Sand, *The Invention of the Jewish People*, op.cit. Ch 5, pp 256-279. Israeli-Jewish "scientists", engage in the same type of pseudo research into "Jewish genes" that their German Nazi counterparts researched on the "Aryan Genes" practiced in the 1930s. Totalitarian ideology guides research in defense of genocide and ethnic expulsion. ZPC objections to the Nazi comparisons would be better directed at Israeli state-funded Jewish gene research.

95   See Albert Lindemann, *Esau's Tears: Modern Anti-Semitism and the Rise of the Jews* (Cambridge (UK): Cambridge University Press 1997) pp. 59. Lindemann's historical survey of the socio-economic position of Jews is a balanced account describing the power, wealth and property of Jews in Europe, as well as their persecution and dispossession. The study puts the lie to the Zionist notion that "Jews" suffered oppression and persecution for 2000 years. The question is: Which *class* of Jews was persecuted in which countries, under which regimes in what time frame. For example Lindemann details the extraordinary political, media, financial and commercial power of Jews in Hungary (Budapest), Austria (Vienna), Germany (Berlin) during the fifty years before the 1920s. See pp. 119, 138, 188, 189-190.

96   Shlomo Sand, *The Invention of the Jewish People*, Ch.2.

97   See James Petras' *Zionism, Militarism and the Decline of US Power* (Atlanta: Clarity Press 2008) Ch 1-2; James Petras, *Rulers and Ruled in the US Empire*, Ch 8, 10.

98   Jeff Blankfort "What the US Elite Really Thinks About Israel" *Counterpunch* 12/8/09.

99   My calculations based on Congressional reports on campaign funding.

100   While liberal critics of the "Israel Lobby" posit a notion of the "national interest" without any clarification of which *class interests* in the nation are central, our perspective defines the national interest in terms of what benefits the wage and salaried classes.

101   See James Petras, *Zionism, Militarism and the Decline of US Power* (Atlanta: Clarity Press, Inc., 2008).

TRASHING AMERICA FOR ISRAEL

THE ZIONIST LOBBY KISSES DUAL LOYALTIES GOODBYE

"The Government of Israel has insulted the Vice President of the United States, and spat in the face of the President … they wiped the spit off their faces and smiled politely … as the saying goes: when you spit in the face of a weakling, he pretends that it is raining"
Uri Avnery, Israeli Jewish journalist
March 13, 2010.

"We (Israel) *possess several hundred atomic warheads and rockets … most European capitals are targets of our air force … the Palestinians should all be deported. Two years ago, only 7 or 8 per cent of Israelis were of the opinion that this would be the best solution, two months ago, (January 2010), it was 33 percent and now according to a Gallup poll, the figure is 44 percent".*
Martin Van Creveld, top adviser to the Israeli Armed Forces
Israeli Professor of Military History,Hebrew University
March 2, 2010

Introduction

When Israel announced a major new *Jews-only* building project of 1600 homes in occupied East Jerusalem during the visit of Vice-President Joseph Biden, it was not only *"spitting in the face"* of the visiting vice president, it was demonstrating its power to *humiliate America* and *Americans.* Netanyahu was sending a message to the entire world, similar to the message that it had just sent to the Arab world by the blatant and undenied Mossad assassination of a Hamas official in Dubai. The message is: Israel, backed by its billionaire-financed Conference of Presidents of Major American Jewish Organizations (CPMAJO), leads the US by the nose. Israel will do as it likes, and there is nothing that can be done. The Jewish State can make an agreement with the White House one day, say on freezing settlements in the Occupied West Bank, and revoke it (with characteristic arrogance—by public announcement and/or simply by act) the next, US public opinion be damned.

No sooner did the Obama Administration react to this most public show of impudence with Biden privately telling the Israeli Prime Minister that, "*What you're doing here undermines the security of our troops who are fighting in Iraq, Afghanistan and Pakistan. That endangers us and it endangers regional peace.*", than Netanyahu brazenly called on the "American Jewish community" (the 51 major Zionist organizations[1]) to come to the defense of Israel and its claim on all of Jerusalem. And respond they did: turning the insulted victim (America) into the bully and blaming the US, not the Israeli government, for the "crisis" and for the breakdown of Israel's agreement not to expand colonial settlements on occupied Palestinian land. As we shall describe, the entire Zionist power configuration in the United States (with a few notable exceptions) defended Israel's effrontery and condemned any attempt by the US government to peacefully resolve a conflict, which threatened US lives, economic interests and prestige. This just confirmed world public opinion, which sees an American Congress willing to be bought and humiliated by this economically insignificant state.

Zionist Power Configuration: How Dare You Resist Humiliation!

Is it any wonder that, when visiting American leaders are openly insulted by the racist regime of Prime Minister 'Bibi' Netanyahu, American Zionists automatically side with Israel and condemn those who protest in defense of American dignity?

The *Daily Alert*, principal bulletin of the Conference of Presidents of Major American Jewish Organizations, provides a useful compilation of the articles, editorials and government documents defending Israel against the US Administration's efforts to seek diplomatic solutions. From March 15–19, 2010 the Israeli-ZPC juggernaut released a remarkable propaganda offensive, vividly underscoring the immense power of the Zionist power configuration in the US. As soon as the White House publicly rebuked Prime Minister Netanyahu for insulting Vice-President Biden during his official visit to Israel, the Zionist power configuration, claiming to speak for all the "Jewish communities", came out in defense of Israel and attacked the Obama Administration. A barrage of articles, editorials and press conferences materialized overnight, with the usual parade of zombie-like Congressional mouthpieces parroting the Zionist line and applying direct pressure on the White House. This multi-prong Zionist offensive, under Netanyahu's direction, was successful in persuading the White House to return to its characteristic belly-crawl: Clinton, Biden and the rest of their gang retreated, reasserting the US *"unconditional defense of Israel"*, declaring the *'non-existence'* of the crisis and asserting the *'rock solid'* American relation with Israel.

The chain of command is revealing: The Israeli state orders the Zionist power configuration into action; the mass media disseminates the line; Congress marches lock-step for the Zionists and the White House retreats. Delighted with their success, Zionist propagandists roll out their own polls claiming the US public support for Israel—a public saturated with Israeli manufactured and American Zionist trumpeted propaganda. *Clearly what such "polls" actually measure is the effectiveness of a monolithic mass media campaign.*

The propaganda tactics utilized in this blitzkrieg media campaign involved placing blame on the insulted victim and attacking "the Administration for sparking a full blown crisis" (*Wall Street Journal*, March 14, 2010). It went on to denounce the US Administration officials for *"condemning"* and *"pushing"* Israel (*Washington Post*, March 15 – 19, 2010). Other publications accused President Obama of *'playing into the hand'* of Arab extremists and *"fanning the flames"* (*Fox News* and *Christian Science Monitor*, March 18, 2010). It was the US President, who had been *"hindering the peace talks"* by *"encouraging Palestinian intransigence"*. *Ha'aretz*, the Israelis' liberal newspaper, which has published articles critical of the Israeli Occupation, released a series of articles, opinion pieces and editorials by 'experts' and 'military strategists' accusing the US Administration of *"orchestrating the crises"* (March 14, 2010) and called for the Israeli government not to *'grovel'* by apologizing to the US Vice President (March 15). CBS claimed that *"Obama was pushing the US-Israeli alliance to the brink"* (March 15). And on March 17, the *Boston Globe* accused Obama of *"aggravating Israel's mistake"*. AIPAC methodically contacted its usual Congressional flunkeys to denounce the White House for rebuking the Israeli government.

By March 19, the *Washington Post* had published over a dozen diatribes calling for US acceptance of Israel's settlement expansion. Zionist think tanks and front groups with deceptive names, like the *Foundation for the Defense of Democracies*, blamed the displaced Palestinians for sabotaging *"the peace process"* by protesting the accelerated Israeli land confiscation and settlements (*Scripps – Howard* and *Fox News*, March 18, 2010). Predictably, *The New York Times* provided a slightly liberal gloss by calling for reconciliation and an end to the crisis, while never mentioning the public Israeli humiliation of Vice-President Biden or considering how Israel's latest grab of Palestinian neighborhoods in East Jerusalem might endanger US lives and interests. The *Times* ignored General Petraeus' testimony before Congress and his briefing, critical of Israeli policy, before the Chairman of the Joint Chiefs of Staff, while giving prominence to Netanyahu's *"peace talks"* (March 18, 2010).

A few fissures appeared in the pro-Israel monolith: David Axelrod,

Obama's chief adviser, condemned Netanyahu's provocation as an "insult"; *The New York Times* top columnist, Thomas Friedman, described the Israeli leaders as "*drunken drivers*"; and a leading US rabbi called for a building freeze in Jerusalem. These few liberal Zionist critics were overwhelmed by scores parroting ZPC '*talking points*' such as Bronner and Sanger of *The New York Times*, Walter Mead of *American* [sic] *Interest* and Goldberg of *The New Yorker*, among others.

The craven capitulation, led by Secretary of State Hillary Clinton, was inevitable. On March 16 Secretary Clinton declared that, "*we have an* absolute *commitment to Israel's security. We have a close unshakeable bond between the United States and Israel and between the American and Israeli people*". To prove her fealty to Israeli and Zionist interests, Clinton became featured speaker at the APAC Conference, March 21 – 26, 2010, sharing the platform with a triumphant Bibi Netanyahu.

The Bigger Issue: Beyond the Biden-Netanyahu Caper

Whatever the insults and crimes of the moment, the conflict between Israel and the US is not about Netanyahu's hyper-arrogance or a new series of Jerusalem land grabs, or even the frothy spittle on Vice-President Biden's face. It is, in essence, about the *relation between states* or, more ominously, the relation between peoples where one group (Israeli Jews and their powerful one percent fifth column *agents* in the US) exacts tribute and imposes wars in its own interests on another group (the American taxpayers, soldiers, workers and businesspeople). Israel has arrogated a vastly disproportionate power within the United States, not merely yesterday or today, but over the last 50 years.

In a broader historic context, the public humiliation of Vice-President Biden in Tel Aviv pales in comparison to the Israelis'coldblooded sneak attack, which killed and wounded over 200 American servicemen on the USS *Liberty* in June 1967. An arrogant and homicidal Israel humiliated the US through this attack, confident that then-President Lyndon Johnson would not retaliate but would even silence the survivors from ever telling their story to the American people. When Netanyahu calls on the "Jewish Communities" in the US he is not referring to the majority of American Jews who are now beginning to turn away from Israel from either distaste or disinterest.[2] He is, in fact, is addressing *the Zionist power configuration* whose strategically-placed members designed and promoted the Iraq war policy, which has caused the deaths and mutilation of thousands of US soldiers as well as of over one million Iraqi civilians—with no end in sight. In essence, the US soldier *victims* of the invasion of Iraq lost their lives, limbs and sanity—not to bring democracy, not to remove a dictator, not even for oil[3]—but to advance the interests of the Zionist "homeland".

It's not just about the individual instances: that American Zionists defend the illegal construction of another Jews-only neighborhood in the middle of Palestinian East Jerusalem—with the announcement was calculated to humiliate the visiting US Vice President; that US Zionists' supported Netanyahu's sabotage of a US peace initiative; that the unconditional ZPC supported Israeli crimes as they were being denounced by the United Nations and the peoples of the world, and compelled the US Congress to do likewise. The fundamental issue is that the ZPC in the United States is turning our country *and its people* into defenders (and indeed, imitators!) of Israel's sordid crimes, casting the American people as accomplices to and participants in ethnic cleansing and degrading our moral sensibilities before the whole world.

Israel's 'Will to Power' Emerges

Netanyahu's symbolic spitting in Biden's face was a calculated act of grave significance. It marked out Israel's 'will to power'—*its willingness to publicly humiliate US leaders and flaunt its power over the US before the world.* Israel exposed US impotence in the Middle East and beyond. This incident has world-historic consequences for anyone who is not blind. The US is a *declining* power, which *cannot* create a secure environment for its soldiers, corporations and citizens anywhere in the Middle East or beyond. No European, Asian, Latin American or Muslim country can look at the US and its citizens without thinking, "*Here is a country at the* feet *of Israeli leaders and at the throat of Israel's designated 'enemies'.* It is an understatement to say that the US, as a nation and as a people, has "lost prestige".

Israel has a long and ignoble history of sabotaging peace talks in favor of grabbing land. From its very foundation, Tel Aviv undermined peace offers through unprovoked military attacks. Israel, along with Britain and France, launched a full-scale surprise invasion of Egypt to grab the Suez Canal, after it had promised to consider Egyptian President Nasser's proposal to negotiate. In more recent times, as soon as Arafat agreed to formally recognize Israel as a state and sign a peace agreement, Jewish tanks and jets attacked the West Bank killing hundreds and surrounding Arafat's headquarters for months. At the same time it increased the number of the Jews-only settlements in the West Bank ten fold to accommodate over 500,000 fanatical paramilitary Jewish *settlers*. When the elected Hamas administration implemented and maintained a unilateral ceasefire, Israel launched a major military assault, ultimately devastating Gaza and killing 1400 mostly unarmed Palestinians.

Israel's actions, past and present, including land grabs, Jews-only apartheid roads and settlements and military invasions of Palestinian refugee camps and towns have destroyed the possibility of a negotiated peace agreement, which would compromise the Zionists' vision of an ethnically-cleansed "Greater Israel".

Given this history, it not surprising that Israel's current apologists claim that the current land grab to build more Jews-only apartment blocks in Jerusalem is *"nothing new"*, that it is *"part of our history"*, that Jews *"need the living space"* and that *"three thousand years of Biblical history tells us that all this land is ours"* (quotes from the *Daily Alert*, March 15-17, 2010, official mouthpiece of the Conference of Presidents of the Major American Jewish Organizations).

The humiliation of Biden was not the first time that Israel acted publicly to embarrass the Obama Administration. In his first meeting with President Obama, Prime Minister Netanyahu openly rejected any freeze in new settlements. Indeed, Israel escalated its settlement building right after Obama addressed the Muslim-Arab world in his 'Cairo Speech'.

What is behind Netanyahu's perverse behavior and his US supporters' overweening arrogance? How can the US media, hundreds of Congressional Representatives and all the leading Jewish American organizations, *support* an extremist racist regime, which attacked and humiliated our country with impunity? How can the American Zionists side with a foreign country over issues detrimental to basic US security interests—as made clear by none other than General Petraeus himself—and not be viewed as traitors by other Americans?

In the first place, Netanyahu has the support of 80% of the Israeli-Jewish population as he pursues the policy of evicting the Palestinians and expanding exclusively Jewish settlements on occupied lands despite US President Obama's 'peace overtures'. Humiliating the visiting US Vice-President on a 'peace mission' from Obama only increased Netanyahu's popularity with Israelis.

Secondly, this impudent projection of Israeli power over the reputed American 'superpower' appeals to the self-image of the far-right religious settlers whose leaders form the backbone of the current governing coalition (especially the Shas party).

Thirdly, insulting a gentile president and vice-president would find approval among the supporters of Netanyahu's gangster Foreign Minister, Avi Lieberman and with the tough Eastern European Hasidic youth who routinely spit on elderly Christian monks and priests in their ancient Armenian and Greek quarters of Jerusalem.

It might seem strange for Israelis, who face increasing isolation throughout the Middle East and are condemned throughout Europe for their brutal colonial crimes, to glorify their thuggish leader as he heaps contempt on their most important military ally and economic supporter, its elected leaders and its citizens. Accumulated Israeli political resentment against world condemnation for their war crimes found an emotional outlet by identifying with Netanyahu's antics: His relentless brutality against the *'Untermenschen'* of Palestine and his willingness to openly defy the US administration, even as Israel extracts $3 billion dollars a year from the Americans, re-enforces their sense of superiority. It is clear that Netanyahu's totalitarian policies have a mass popular base among Israelis and his swaggering arrogance faithfully reflects the national psyche of Israel as it now stands.

Netanyahu and his ministers calculated that no matter how hard they squeeze the hapless US taxpayers, themselves caught in the a profound economic crisis, and no matter how often the Israelis threaten to provoke a wider regional war and cause more American soldier casualties, to say nothing of the vastly greater casualties inflicted on the civilian populations of the target states, they can always count on the unconditional support of the Zionist Power Configuration[4] in the US to promote Israel's interest. The major Zionist leaders all rushed to support Israel's humiliation of the US and to denigrate its critics. Worse, the entire US mass media applauded the Great Humiliator and even attacked the few American public figures as they (at least temporarily) defended American dignity against Israeli insults. An endless parade of US politicians, editorial writers, columnists, opinion-makers, "think" tankers, and TV commentators *demonstrated their special loyalty to Israel* against an American president who was timidly seeking a negotiated peace in the Middle East.

The recent 'conflict' between Israel and America over peace in the Middle East—brought on by the crude Israeli provocation—exposed far more profound issues: at the center of power in America, there is an influential group of power-brokers willing to exploit and humiliate the American people in the service of a foreign power. In the past, patriots would have called them 'traitors'.

Netanyahu's Hubris 'Rebuked'

In response to the official Washington *show* of anger, Netanyahu issued a half-hearted "*explanation*": The problem was *not* the *policy* of building new settlements *in violation* of the Israeli government's agreement with Washington; the problem was the *timing* of the announcement. It was a regrettable "*error*" by a minor functionary in the Israeli Interior Ministry who made his announcement right *after* US Vice-President Biden had finished groveling at Netanyahu's feet and was busy pressuring the Palestinian Authority collaborators to rejoin the '*peace'* charade sponsored by Washington. According to the Israeli media and their US mouthpieces it was a *public relations breakdown*, not a matter of strategic political and military significance affecting the US in the Middle East. In other words: With Biden out of Israel and collaborator Abbas back at the 'table', any *announcement* violating the "freeze on settlements" would be merely an Israeli "internal policy" and a "continuation of past practices".

Netanyahu Comes to Washington: Backhanders for Obama, Cheers from AIPAC

Invigorated by spitting on Vice-President Biden in Tel Aviv, Netanyahu administered a series of humiliating 'back-handed' slaps in the smiling face of President Obama, right under the glaring lights of the mass media in the US capital.

Bibi Netanyahu delivered a rabble rousing speech to over 7,000 cheering Zionists at the annual AIPAC conference in Washington, DC. He asserted Israel's will to construct *Jews-only* housing throughout occupied Arab East Jerusalem and the West Bank, repeating Israel's illegal claim that Jerusalem was the undivided capital of the Jewish people. He then demanded and secured a two-hour meeting with Obama, despite his arrogant insult against the US Administration. Adding further humiliation to the already weak US President, the Israel government then announced *another Jews-only* housing project in Arab East Jerusalem to be built on confiscated Palestinian property. This announcement, just hours before the planned Bibi-Barack meeting, carried an additional threat that the White House charade of *'peace negotiations'* would be put off the table if the Americans protested this new round of illegal construction. Netanyahu, demonstrating his utter contempt for the White House and the America people, went straight to the Zion-colonized US Congress and secured the House Majority leader Pelosi's *'unconditional support...'* for Israeli expansion. And, as if to celebrate its victory and establish its own definition of *'peace'*, the Israeli military assassinated four unarmed Palestinians, two impoverished job-seekers and two young teenage protesters.

Loyalty to the Israeli masters was evident when thousands of Zionist fanatics jumped to their feet and cheered Bibi Netanyahu's crude repudiation of the American efforts to protect its soldiers' lives by promoting a peace initiative. Hillary Clinton's call for a *'peace settlement based on two states for two people'* was met with dead silence. The entire Zionist-dominated media and all the leading Jewish organizations backed an unprecedented series of humiliations directed against the elected US Administration and the American people. Netanyahu's demagogic display of Israeli power over the US Congress and the American mass media and his crude willingness to degrade US political leaders in the nation's capital mocks the very notion of the American people having any voice in their nation's policies and even subordinates America's military high command over issues of war and peace in the Middle East.

For Pelosi and the Zionized Congress, the thousands of campaign shekels from the AIPAC crowd to fund their re-elections are far more crucial to their careers than the lives and limbs of thousands of US soldiers lost to an agenda of Israel and its domestic Fifth Column—or indeed, than the inevitable further degradation of the American economy and military, impacting American life thereby in all its dimensions.

Israel's Arrogance Prejudices US Interests

Israel's leaders not only raised their domestic prestige by undermining the US Administration's peace initiatives, they also managed to extract billions of dollars from the US taxpayers. The humiliation of the Obama regime derailed efforts by the Pentagon and the State Department to regain influence and credibility among the conservative Arab regimes, non-Arab Muslim nations and among hundred of millions of Muslims around the world. This humbling of the US Administration by a sneering Netanyahu further jeopardizes the work and security of American businessmen and officials operating in the Middle East and elsewhere, and undermines relations with their Muslim and Arab counterparts.

There will be major setbacks for the US in its efforts to gain support for its wars in the Middle East and South Asia and its propaganda campaign to discourage young Muslims everywhere from joining the anti-US resistance in Iraq, Afghanistan and Somalia. The symbolic image of the American vice president wiping away Israeli spittle during an official visit will encourage thousands of young Muslims to resist US occupation, which they view as promoting Israel's agenda. If an economically insignificant Israeli state can defy the superpower, why can't they? The logic is simple: The greater the Israeli land-grab, the more submissive the Obama regime, the more extended and profound the hostility of the Muslim people against the Americans, the more emboldened the armed resistance movements and the greater the number of dead and maimed American soldiers stuck in wars promoted by the Zionists.

While the losses of American soldiers in the Middle East have never figured in Tel Aviv's policy moves, nor influenced the activities of its Fifth Colum in the USA, these losses do affect millions of American families and over 200 million American taxpayers. It's gotten to the point that even an occasional American general finds the courage to point out that Israel's colonial dispossession of the Palestinian people has prolonged the war, tied up hundreds of thousands of US troops and undermined the capacity of the US armed forces to successfully operate on multiple fronts to promote US imperial interests.

When his team of senior officers identified "*Israeli intransigence*" as "*jeopardizing US standing and the lives of American soldiers in the region (Middle East)*" in a briefing before the Chairman of the Joint Chiefs of Staff on January 16, 2010, the head of the US Central Command (CENTCOM), General Petraeus, faced an onslaught of severe questioning from the ZPC. The Chairman of the Joint

Chiefs, Admiral Mullens, received the same rebuke from the powerful Israel-Firsters. This was not the first time US military and security considerations were subsumed to Israel's agenda. Only two years earlier in 2007, the *ZPC* denounced and successfully buried the annual National Intelligence Estimate (NIE) prepared by 16 US military and civilian intelligence agencies, which had concluded that Iran was not developing nuclear weapons and did not pose a major threat to the US, in favor of Israeli disinformation arguing the opposite. Needless to say, the same ZPC has been taking the Obama regime to task for daring to criticize Netanyahu.

Over *300 members* of the US Congress signed an extraordinary letter supporting Israel against their own Administration, pledging their commitment to *"the unbreakable bond that exists between [U.S.] and the State of Israel"*. Hundreds of Congress people and officials joined the over 7,000 participants at the March 2010 AIPAC conference to cheer Netanyahu and witness the US Secretary of State Hilary Clinton hail the leader of the Israeli settler state—who had pledged *"to continue building in all of Jerusalem just as it does in Tel Aviv"*.

General David Petraeus, whose senior officers had expressed his concern about Israel's policies undermining US military interests to Chairman of the Joint Chiefs of Staff, Admiral Mullins, was no match for the AIPAC. The CENTCOM commander contacted his Israeli counterpart, General Gabi Ashkenazi, to repudiate his own criticism of Israeli policies and, in effect, pledge his unconditional support to the Jewish state even when it jeopardizes US troops.

In January, General Petraeus had correctly identified how Israeli intransigence had damaged US interests and operations in the Middle East, infuriated Arabs and ultimately increased attacks on American troops. But in March, the politically ambitious General hastened to retract his briefing before the Joint Chiefs of Staff. There are few more cravenly disloyal spectacles in US military history than that of this bemedaled American general prostrating himself before the Zionist lobby.

For a brief moment, a few desperate anti-Zionists leftists, myself included, looked to General Petraeus and Admiral Mullen as potential *allies* (or in my case, a last line of defense within the American body politic) against Israeli-Zionist control of US policy in the Middle East. They ignored the fact that these are the commanders in charge of the US invasion and occupation of Iraq and Afghanistan and were preparing to confront Iran—two of which engagements, at least, are at Israeli/ZPC behest. Petraeus' difference with Israel was over *specific* policies as they *undermined* the smooth operations of the US war machine in the Middle East and his 'recantation' before the Israelis has certainly thrown cold water on this romantic fantasy of a 'nationalist' US general.

The tradition of 'civilian supremacy' in the US ensures that the military will never confront the issue of Zionist control over the Congress and White House. Petraeus' briefing will be soon forgotten and the General's subsequent repudiation is an eloquent example of the grotesquely opportunistic nature of the American high military command.

When civilian leaders point out how Israel's oppression of five million Palestinians jeopardizes American lives and interests in the Middle East, the Zionist power configuration deflects attention from Israel and blames the US (and its 'permissive' society) for having instigated the growing Islamist movement, Arab hostility and attacks. When American military leaders, strategists and intelligence officers assert that Israel's policy toward the Palestinians is a leading cause of regional conflict based on their decades of field expertise, the armchair generals among the Zionists re-interpret this straightforward identification of Israeli policy with attacks on American interests and troops as "*another point of view*". In the meantime the ZPC rounds up the usual Congressional or White House *Israel Firsters* to "disown" their own military.

Israel's narrowly conceived colonial policy, the eviction of massive numbers of Palestinians and the land grabs to construct Jews-only colonial settlements, undermines US authority in the Middle East among its non-Arab, non-Muslim allies as well. Israel's brazen willingness and ability to openly bash President Obama, thoroughly discredits the contention among liberal Zionist apologists like Noam Chomsky that *Imperial* Washington is "in command" of Western policy in the Middle East and is acting on behalf of much broader Euro-American interests.

In a wider context, Israel's arrogance damages attempts by US private investors to broker oil deals for multinational corporations. Arab oil countries, which see themselves as threatened by a regional militarist power like Israel, with its colonial expansion and hegemonic ambitions, are unlikely to cooperate with the Americans, especially when the superpower is impotent to curb Israel's worst excesses.

Israeli Colonial Ambitions and US Strategic Interests

For Israel and its Fifth Column backers none of the US strategic concerns are as important as the Jewish state's colonial conquests and its regional projections of power. Nor are the interests of the American people given much consideration when they come in conflict with Israeli expansionist colonial goals. The ZPC never considers or even discusses the fact that Americans have suffered major losses as a result of Israel's relentless pursuit of military-driven power in the Middle East.

Israel's primary goal of grabbing land and dispossessing Palestinians goes against the post-colonial ethos of the American people, who experience increased hostility overseas. The only beneficiaries of Israel colonial expansion are the small but powerful 51 American Jewish Zionist organizations which identify with and are loyal to the Israeli state.

Israel's unilateral military aggression and threats against neighboring countries, including Palestine, Syria, Lebanon, Iran and its cross-border covert assassinations, most recently in Dubai, are of great importance to Israeli militarists as Israel projects power in the Middle East. The self-esteem of Israel's militarized citizens is directly linked to their policy of aggression and assassinations without regard to national sovereignty. On the other hand, Israeli power projections have undermined the US efforts to *diplomatically* expand its own sphere of influence and negotiate multi-billion dollar military sales, trade and investment agreements in the Middle East. The fact that Israeli policies have jeopardized millions of jobs for American workers is an issue of no importance to the Jewish state and its affluent Israel First backers in the US.

Israel's invasion of Lebanon forced the pro-US Harari faction to form a coalition with the anti-imperialist Hezbollah political-military movement. Israel's attempt to impose its will on Lebanon through its bombing campaign, torpedoed US diplomatic and political efforts to consolidate its influence with President Harari.

Netanyahu's successful bullying of Obama and Biden simply reinforced the ties between the pro-Western Lebanese and the anti-colonial Muslim left, in the face of Washington's incapacity to constrain the Israeli 'wildmen' or resist the 'internal rot' eroding an independent American initiative: Better to join forces with Hezbollah, which after all fought Israel to a standstill in 2006.

Israel's loyal accomplices in the US government have caused enormous damage to the US economy and threaten even greater loss of American lives, as the Israel seeks to direct US policy toward Iran. Under the forceful and aggressive direction of Israel Firsters and the powerful Treasury Undersecretary for Terrorism and Financial Intelligence, Stuart Levey, every major US oil and gas company, bank, petroleum exploration and drilling firms and countless other business concerns have given up hundreds of billion dollars in lucrative economic trade an investment deals in the interest of Israel, which has extracted over $60 billion dollars of US taxpayer money and handouts and aid during the last decade. And when the government failed to sufficiently enforce the embargo it is encouraging worldwide against its own US companies doing business in Iran, *The New York Times* was there to make sure the malfeasance was exposed.[5]

Iran, which backed the US imperial attacks on Afghanistan and Iraq, provided the US military with far more strategic assistance than all the Israeli advisers, 'experts' and contracted 'interrogators' in

Baghdad and Iraqi 'Kurdistan' put together. Despite the US recognition of Iranian assistance in Iraq and Afghanistan, Iran is demonized as 'the enemy' by Israeli agents within the US because Tehran opposes Israel's ethnic cleansing of the Palestinians. Israel's Fifth Column churns out hundreds of articles a month demanding brutal economic sanctions against Iran and a pre-emptive military blitz aimed at destroying the Iranian economy and a nation of over 70 million. Every US military commander in the Middle East has acknowledged that an attack on Iran will expand the war, cut vital shipping of oil in the Persian Gulf plunging the world economy into recession, and threaten the lives of scores of *thousands* of American soldiers.

Conclusion

Israel had to openly humiliate the US in order to demonstrate its power to the world. Given Israel's strategic domination of the US political system and the ZPC control over mass media and their enormous wealth, an administration, like Obama's, already Zionist-controlled, would have to capitulate. Israeli and US Zionist pressure forced the American leaders to subordinate their international image and national self-respect and accept the unlimited expansion of Jews-only settlements in the West Bank and East Jerusalem, no matter how this might undermine US standing in the region and jeopardize US troops. By publicly 'whipping' the Obama Administration into line, Israel has set the stage for the launching of its top priority: a direct US military confrontation with Iran in Israel's strategic interests. It is clear that the entire ZPC will stand with Israel as it promotes its militarist agenda against Iran, regardless of the consequences to the United States.

It has been proved beyond a doubt by the recent events, that the ZPC has the ultimate say with the Obama Administration, possibly against the personal inclination of the president, himself, and assuredly against the advice of top US military officials and against the basic interests of the American people. In plain English, we Americans are a people colonized and directed by a small, extremist and militarist 'ally' which operates through domestic proxies who are citizens of our country, who, under any other circumstance, would be openly denounced as traitors.

Can the ZPC be defeated? They are the "most powerful lobby in Washington", to whom presidents, administration officials, generals and Congress people must submit or risk having their careers ruined and being ousted from public office.[6] Meanwhile, outside of the United States, a large part of the international community openly despises Israel as a brutal, racist, colonial state, a chronic violator of human rights and international law, a perpetrator of war crimes, and possibly even crimes against humanity. The Middle East Quartet, made up of the United States, the European Union, Russia and the United Nations, has condemned Israel's plan to build another 1,600 homes exclusively for Jewish extremist settlers in Arab East Jerusalem. The Quartet demanded "the *speedy creation of a Palestinian state and the end to provocative actions*". But the 'Quartet' is powerless to stop Israeli plans. Even as the Presidents of the 51 Major American Jewish Organizations tell their followers that *global "anti-Semitism"* motivates the 'Quartet', the huge AIPAC "Hail Israel" Conference in Washington D.C. in late March celebrated the triumph of unfettered Israeli expansionism.

Nevertheless, some Israelis are beginning to express unease. After their initial euphoria over Netanyahu's slap-down of Biden and face-up to Clinton, there is growing fear of Israeli being '*weaned*' away from the depleted American treasury and losing their unfettered access to the US latest military technology. A poll published on March 19 in *Yedroth Ahronoth*, one of Israel's biggest dailies, revealed that 46% of their readers responded that the government should freeze settlement building in East Jerusalem, much to the chagrin of the US Israel Firsters, who might in other circumstances, have labeled these Israeli Jews anti-Semites.

Fissures in the Zionist monolith are beginning to appear. These would deepen if and when the American public realized that Israel's' dispossession of Palestinians is against Israel's own interests. What future is there for Israel, on the back of Palestinian apartheid, ethnic cleansing or genocide—and mounting global hatred? As more issues arise, the critical choice for Americans between following the lead of the ZPC in pledging unconditional allegiance to Israel and enduring its provocations and humiliations, *or* standing up for the dignity, basic interests and integrity of the United States, will have to be made. More fissures will appear and the AIPAC and other members of the ZPC will be seen for what they are: *Swaggering bullies acting on behalf of a foreign power. An American fifth column.*

Endnotes

1   For a list of the 51 organizations, see Chapter 11 in James Petras, *Global Depression and Regional Wars*, Clarity Press, Inc., Atlanta, 2009.

2   For a more extensive analysis of the changing views of Jewish Americans, see Norman Silverstein, *This Time We Went Too Far*, Or Books, 2010. <http://www.orbooks.com >

3   For an analysis of the primary role of US Zionists and Israeli interests in instigating the war on Iraq and a critique of the "alternative" Big Oil theories, see James Petras, *The Power of Israel in the United States*, Clarity Press, Inc., 2006.

4   See Chapter 1, James Petras, *Zionism, Militarism and the*

Decline of US Power, Clarity Press, Atlanta, 2008.
5   See Jo Becker, "US Enriches Companies Defying Its Policy on Iran," *The New York Times*, March 6, 2010, < http://www.nytimes.com/2010/03/07/world/middleeast/07sanctions.html>.
6   See endnote 4.

MOSSAD'S MURDEROUS REACH

THE IMPLICATIONS OF
THE DUBAI ASSASSINATION

On January 19, 2010, Israel's international secret police, the Mossad, sent an 26 member death squad to Dubai using European passports, supposedly 'stolen' from Israeli dual citizens and altered with fake photos and signatures, in order to assassinate the Palestinian leader, Mahmoud al Mabhouh in one of the world's luxurious hotels, frequented by a global clientele.

The evidence implicating Israel was overwhelming: The Dubai police presentation of detailed security videos of the assassins was corroborated by the testimony of Israeli security experts and applauded by Israel's leading newspapers and columnists. The Mossad openly stated that Mabhouh was a high priority target who had survived three previous assassination attempts. Israel did not even bother to deny the murder. Furthermore, the sophisticated communication system used by the killers, the logistics and planning surrounding their entry and exit from Dubai, and the scope and scale of the operation have all the characteristics of a high-level state operation. Furthermore, only Mossad would have access to the European passports of its dual citizens! Only Mossad would have the capacity, motivation, stated intent and willingness to provoke a diplomatic row with its European allies, knowing full well that Western European governments' anger would blow over because of their deep links to Israel. After meticulous investigation and the interrogation of 2 captured Palestinian Mossad collaborators, the Dubai police chief has stated he is sure the Mossad was behind the killing. The authorities in Dubai found clear evidence that the Mossad assassination team received support from European Zionists. The hotels, air tickets and expenses were paid for with credit cards issued in the US. Two of the killers may be in the US now.

The Larger Political Issues

Israel's policy of extra-territorial assassinations raises profound issues that threaten the basis of the modern state: *sovereignty, rule of law, and national and personal security.*

Israel has a publicly-stated policy of violating the *sovereignty* of any and all countries in order to kill or abduct its opponents. In both proclamation and actual practice, the Israeli state regards its own law, decrees and actions abroad as superseding the laws and law enforcement agencies of any other nation—to say nothing of international law. If Israel's policy becomes the common practice worldwide, we would enter a savage Hobbesian jungle in which individuals would be subject to the murderous intent of foreign assassination squads unrestrained by any law or accountable national authority. State governments would become the equivalent of warlords or gangsters, with each and every state imposing its own laws and crossing national borders in order to murder and despoil other nation's citizens or residents and their resources with impunity.

Israel's *extra-territorial assassinations* make a mockery of the very notion of national sovereignty—and they are not without precedent. Extra-territorial secret police elimination of opponents was a common practice of the Nazi Gestapo, Stalin's GPU, apartheid-era South Africa, and Pinochet's DINA and has now become the sanctioned practice of the US "Special Forces" and the CIA clandestine division. Indeed, the US military has now taken it one step further, asserting the right to extra-territorial assassination of *its own American citizens.* Such policies are the hallmark of totalitarian, dictatorial and imperialist states, which systematically trample on the sovereign rights of peoples.

Israel's practice of extra-judicial, extra-territorial assassinations, exemplified by the recent murder of Mahmoud al Mabhouh in a Dubai hotel room, violates all the fundamental precepts of the rule of law. *Extra-judicial killings* ordered by a state, mean its own secret police are judge, jury, prosecutor and executioner, unrestrained by sovereignty, law and the duty of nations to protect their citizens and visitors. Evidence, legal procedures, defense and cross examinations are obliterated in the process. State-sponsored, extra-judicial murder completely undermines due process. Liquidation of opponents abroad is the logical next step after Israel's domestic application of its racial laws and administrative detention decrees, which have dispossessed the Palestinian people and violated international laws.

Mossad death squads operate directly under the Israeli Prime Minister (who personally approved the recent murder).The vast majority of Israelis proudly support these assassinations, especially when the killers escape detection and capture. The unfettered operation of foreign state-sponsored death squads, carrying out extra-judicial assassinations with impunity, is a serious threat to every critic, writer, political leader and civic activist who dares to criticize Israel.

The entrenched Israeli policy and practice of extra-judicial killing of its adversaries abroad *establishes the outer boundaries of repression that its overseas supporters* in the leading Zionist organizations are willing to endorse. Most have now and in the past supported Israel's violation of national sovereignty via extra-judicial killings. Heretofore, while Israel physically eliminated its opponents and critics, the modus operandi of the 51 major American Jewish organizations was to attack the livelihoods and reputations of Israel's critics in the US, actively pressuring employers, university presidents and public officials to fire employees, academics and professionals who dare to speak or write against Israeli torture, killing and systematic dispossession of Palestinians.

But with the assassination in Dubai, the outer boundary of that tactic of repression appears to have changed. As the *Daily Alert* again geared up to justify and defend an Israeli outrage, the primary media organ of the Conference of Presidents of Major Jewish Organizations sought not only to defend and justify extra-judicial killings in foreign sovereign states, but to make Mossad practice palatable to Americans.

Mossad Comes to America

The principal propaganda mouthpiece of the Conference of Presidents of Major American Jewish Organizations (CPMAJO), the *Daily Alert* (DA), came out in full support for Israel's practice of extra-judicial, extra-territorial assassination in flagrant disregard of worldwide governmental condemnation (except from the Zionist-occupied White House and US Congress). It slavishly *defended* all of Mossad's criminal actions leading up to the murder, including extensive identity theft and the stealing or falsification of passports and official documents from several European countries, presumably allied to the Zionist state. Of the 26 Mossad agents who entered Dubai to kill Mabhouh, twelve agents were equipped with numerous stolen or forged passports: not only British passports, but three Australian, three French, one German and six Irish.

To put it in its simplest terms: these agents assumed the identity of European citizens in order to commit murder in a sovereign nation.

Once again the CPMAJO demonstrated that its first loyalty is to the Israeli secret police, even when they violate the sovereignty of major US allies. No doubt the CPMAJO would readily support the Israeli Mossad, even if it were shown to have used *US* documents to assassinate Mabhouh. In fact, as mentioned above, two of the 26 Israeli assassins, carrying fake Irish and fake British passports, are known to have entered the United States after the killing and may still be here.

The position adopted by the *Daily Alert* and the CPMAJO in defense of Israel's international terrorist act followed several often contradictory lines of attack *trivializing* and *relativizing* world condemnation. These include:

(1) deflecting attention from the Zionists by blaming *'other Arabs*, (2) blaming the victim, (3) seeking to discredit the Dubai police investigators rather than the Israeli perpetrators, (4) citing "self-defense", and claiming that extra-judicial, extra territorial murders are legal, (5) minimizing the murder by favorably comparing Mossad assassinations to US killings in Afghanistan, and (6) praising the high-tech *'operational details'* of the assassination

Abridged articles, cited in the *Daily Alert*, have since appeared in the op-ed pages of several US, UK, Canadian and Israeli newspapers, as well as in rightwing magazines like *Forbes* and *Commentary*. The mainline Zionist propaganda technique is to avoid any discussion of Israel's egregious crimes against *sovereignty, due process, international law* and the personal security of individuals. In doing so, the *Daily Alert* adopts the propaganda techniques common to all totalitarian regimes practicing state terrorism.

1) Blaming the Arabs: Deflecting Attention from Israel

The *DA* Feb. 22 article entitled *"The Assassination Heard Around the World"* insinuates that the murder was a *"result of a Hamas power struggle"* or by one of *"many Arab groups who loathe the Islamist Hamas"*.

In other words, all the forged or stolen European passports of Israeli dual citizens were somehow procured by "Arab groups" (which, if true ought to have raised a security scandal in Israel). The Dubai security videos of Mossad operatives in various costumes, not to mention the jubilant affirmation by top Israeli leaders of the killing, were in reality *'Arab tricks'*. This crude propaganda ploy by the most prominent Jewish American organization reveals its own descent into a fantasy land of self-delusion, possible only in the closed world of US Zionist politics.

2) Blaming the Victim

On February 22, the *Daily Alert* (DA) headlined two articles, which were entitled: *"Killed Hamas Official betrayed by Associates says Dubai Police Chief"* and *"Hamas: Assassinated Operative put Himself at Risk"*. The *DA* omitted mentioning that Israeli secret police had been tracking their prey for over a month (having failed to assassinate him on six previous attempts) and that the Dubai Police Chief was not blaming Hamas officials but rather was in the process of accumulating evidence, witness statements, videos and documents proving the Israeli identities of the assassins. Needless to say, if we were to accept the American Zionists' argument that any leading opponent of Israel, who travels without an army of bodyguards, is *"putting himself at risk"*, then we must acknowledge that ours is a lawless world where Israeli hit squads are free to commit murder anywhere, any time.

3) Discrediting the Investigators While Defending the Perpetrators

The *DA* on Feb. 25 cited a long and tendentious attack on the Dubai police, published in *Forbes Magazine*, which ridiculed their meticulous investigations uncovering Mossad's role in the murder. In this article, the Dubai authorities were condemned for uncovering Israeli involvement while not investigating the source of the murder victim's ... Iraqi passport! Instead of encouraging the Dubai police pursuit of justice, the *Daily Alert* published a long diatribe implicating Dubai in the attacks of 9/11/2001, condemning its continued trade with Iran, its 'involvement' in international terrorism etc. There was no mention of Dubai's relatively friendly position to Israel and Israelis prior to Mossad's blatant violation of its sovereignty.

4) Extra-Judicial, Extra territorial Murder is "Legal"
(At least, if the killers are Mossad)

The February 22 and February 24 issues of the *DA* include two articles arguing that Israel's practice of extra-judicial, extra-territorial murder is legal. One article is entitled, *"The Legality of Killing of Hamas Mahmoud al Mabhoud"* and the other, *"The Proportionate Killing of Mahmoud al Mabhoud"*. Both avoid any reference to international law, which emphatically rejects cross-border, state-sponsored murders. *Legality*, for the CPMAJO, is whatever the Israel's secret police apparatus deems expedient in pursuit of its goal of eliminating leaders who oppose its colonial occupation and expropriation of Palestinian lands. If Israel's extra-judicial, extra-territorial murder of an adversary in Dubai is legal, why not assassinate opponents in the US, Canada, England or any other country where they might travel, live, work or write? What if the critics and opponents of Israel decided that it was now *"legal"* to murder Israel's supporters wherever they lived, citing the *Daily Alert*'s definition of legality? We would then find ourselves in a lawless world of *"legal"* murder and totalitarian cross-border surveillance.

5) Minimizing the Murder

The Feb 22, 24, and 25 issues of the *Daily Alert* deflect attention from the Mossad murder by making comparison to the hundreds of Afghan civilians killed by US drone attacks. The claim is that *"targeting individuals"* is less a crime than mass killings. The problem with this argument is that for decades Mossad has *"targeted"* scores of opponents overseas and killed thousands of Palestinians in the Occupied Territories (where they work with the domestic secret police, Shin Bet, and the military, IDF). Moreover, this argument linking Israel's extra judicial assassinations with US colonial killing of Afghans is hardly a defense of either. By implicating the US in its defense of state terror, Israel is holding up the worst aspects of American imperialism as a standard for its own political behavior. One state's crimes are no justification for another's.

That Israel can so easily minimize these murders is a testament to the virulence of racism and Islamophobia currently afflicting the western world. What if these murders were carried out against— Swedes, Australians, Canadians...even WASP Americans? Is it conceivable that, as the degradation runs amok, we will eventually get there? Already in America, it has been possible, and even by a so-called progressive magazine like *Mother Jones*, to blame a white American, Rachel Corrie, for her own death by an Isrsaeli bulldozer as she attempted to deflect the demolition of a Palestinian home.

6) Technical Proficiency

Ignoring the fact that it had earlier accused *Arabs* of having committed the crime, the *DA* then published several articles praising the technical details of the assassination, exposing thereby their true beliefs as to who the perpetrators were. The Feb. 24 *DA* article entitled, *"Assassination Shows Skillful Planning"* chastises Israel's critics for not recognizing the high quality of the *"operational aspects"* of the killings and recommends its *"lessons for all intelligence services around the world"*.

It is more likely, however, that most services, including the Mossad, would have regarded the public exposure not of one, three, or ten, but of 26 agents engaged in an assassination in another country as an operation that was incredibly botched—unless, indeed, the public exposure of this exceptionally large number of deployed agents effectively swarming a single, unprotected, targeted person *was intended as a message to the world at large*. Like sociopaths and serial killers, US Zionists openly promote Israeli death squad techniques to all fellow state terrorists as something to be proud of. In the *DA*, professional techniques of assassination are far more important than universal moral repugnance at political murders.

Conclusion

The American Zionist propaganda campaign in defense of Israeli state terror and, specifically, Mossad's murder of a Hamas leader in Dubai, relies on lies, evasions and specious legal arguments. This "defense" violates all precepts of a civilized society as well as the most recent American federal laws prohibiting all forms of support for international terrorism. The CPMAJO can pursue its defense of Mossad's acts of international terrorism with impunity in the US because of its power over the US Congress, the Obama White House and the American mass media. This ensures that only its version of events, its definition of legality and its lies will be heard by legislators, echoed by Zionist activists and embellished by its solemn defenders in academic and journalistic circles. To counter the American Zionist defense of Israel's practice of extra-territorial, extra-judicial executions by the Mossad, we need American writers and academics to step forward. It is time to expose their flimsy arguments, bold-face lies and audacious immorality. It is time to speak out against their impunity, before another Israeli secret police murder takes place, *possibly inside the USA itself* and with the shameless complicity of Zionist accomplices.

Will a time come when American Zionists, who are unconditional public defenders of Mossad killings, cross the line between propaganda *for* the deed to become accomplices *of* the deed? The robust American Zionist defense of Mossad's overseas assassinations does not augur well for the security of Americans in the face of Israel's willing U.S. accomplices.

ISRAELI WAR CRIMES

FROM THE U.S.S. LIBERTY
TO THE HUMANITARIAN FLOTILLA

Introduction: Israel Crimes on the High Seas

On June 8, 1967, two squadrons of Israeli warplanes bombed, napalmed and machine-gunned the US intelligence-gathering ship, U.S.S. *Liberty*, in international waters, killing 34 US sailors and wounding another 172. The assault took place on a sunny afternoon, with the US flag and identifying markers clearly visible. The Israelis targeted the antennae to prevent the crew from broadcasting for help and shot up the lifeboats to ensure no survivors. There were, however, survivors who rigged up an antenna and radioed their distress, a call for help that reached Washington D.C. In an unprecedented act of betrayal, President Johnson, in close liaison with powerful American Jewish Zionist political backers, covered up the mass murder on the high seas by issuing orders first to recall Mediterranean-based warplanes from rushing to assist their besieged comrades, then threatening to court-martial the survivors who might expose the deliberate nature of the Israeli assault and finally by repeating the Israeli line that the attack was a matter of mistaken identity, a lie which numerous military leaders later rejected.

Almost to the day, 43 years later, on May 31, 2010, Israeli warships, helicopter gunships and commandos assaulted a convoy of humanitarian ships carrying ten thousand tons of aid to Gaza in international waters. Prior to the aid mission Turkish authorities had examined the passengers and the ship to ensure no weapons were on board. The Israelis nevertheless came on board shooting and clubbing the unarmed passengers, killing 9 and wounding dozens. Despite subsequent Israeli and Zionist claims to the contrary no weapons were found, apart from sticks used by some of the victims attempting to fend off the murderous premeditated assault planned and directed by top Israeli leaders and defended by the entire leadership of the major Zionist organizations in the US and elsewhere. The invading Israeli storm troopers systematically destroyed all cameras, videos and tape recorders that had documented their savage assault, in order to subsequently spread their brazen lies about their being subject to armed resistance.

The World Response

Within hours of Israel's bloody act of piracy, nations, political leaders, human rights organizations and the vast majority of the international community condemned the Israeli state for its violation of international law. Turkey, Spain, Greece, Denmark and Austria summoned their Israeli ambassadors to protest the deadly assault. The Financial Times, (June 1, 2010) referred to the Israeli assault as a "brazen act of piracy ... hurtling into lawlessness" rooted in its "illegal blockage of Gaza". Turkey's Prime Minister Recep Erdogan called the Israeli assault an act of "state terrorism" which would have "serious consequences". Israel's attacks on ships flying Turkish, Greek and Irish flags on the high seas were described by legal experts as an "act of war". The UN Security Council, NATO and the Secretary General of the UN demanded Israel cease its aggression, while tens of thousands of demonstrators marched denouncing Israel's blatant act of state murder and wounding of pacifists, humanitarians and protestors from 60 countries. UN experts demanded that Israeli leaders "must be held criminally responsible". Only the Obama regime refused to condemn the Israeli act of state terror, merely expressing "concern and regret". The Israeli state defended its murderous assault, promised more in the future and insisted on maintaining its blockade of Gaza, even after the US suggested it might be loosened.

The Israeli Defense of Piracy and State Terror

As news of the Israeli massacre slipped out and the international community reacted with horror and anger, the Israeli government "sought to flood the airwaves with their versions of events ... more importantly, the authorities ensured that their narrative gained early dominance by largely silencing the hundreds of activists who were on board during the attack".[1] The Jewish state held all the prisoners alive, wounded and dead incommunicado, seized their mobile phones and prohibited any interviews, barring all journalists. Like most terrorist states, the Jewish state wanted to monopolize media coverage of the event. The Israeli propaganda machine via its state sponsored journalists and news media employed several ploys typical of totalitarian regimes.

1. Israeli storm troopers invading the ship were turned into victims and the humanitarian pacifists were turned into *aggressors*. "Israeli Soldiers

Met by Well-Planned Lynch Mob".[2]

2. Israel's act of piracy in international waters was declared legal by a Professor Sabel of the Hebrew University.

3. The humanitarian organizers were accused of having ties to terrorists according to Deputy Foreign Minister Ayalon, though no evidence was presented.[3] The organizers including the Turkish human rights group accused by Ayalon were cleared by the Turkish intelligence agency, the military and the Erdogan government, a member of NATO and for many years (in the past) a collaborator with the Israeli Mossad. The other 600 plus human rights volunteers, included pacifists, parliamentarians, former diplomats, as well as current members of the Israeli parliament.

4. While dozens of human rights people were shot, killed and maimed, Israeli propagandists doctored video releases portraying one of the Israeli *assailants* on the deck, cutting out the preceding sequence of their attack on the unarmed peace activists.[4]

5. The Israeli sea and airborne assailants were described as the victims of a "Brutal Ambush at Sea".[5]

6. The terrorized human rights workers were accused of being a "lynch mob", attacking the Jewish commandos who were firing automatic rifles wildly across the deck and at cornered victims. The few courageous individuals who fought back to stop the murderous attack were slandered by the Zion-prop, which itself is as monstrous as the crimes they perpetrated.

Once the Israeli propaganda machine started spewing out its gutter lies, the entire leadership of the Zionist Fifth column swung into action ... first and foremost in the United States.

The US Zionist Power Configuration: In Defense of the Massacre

Just as the entire leadership of the 51 principal American Jewish organizations has defended every Israeli war crime in the past, from the bombing of the U.S.S. *Liberty,* to the occupation of the West Bank and the blockade of Gaza so too did these most honorable apologists repeat verbatim the lies of the Israeli state regarding the assault of the humanitarian flotilla.

The Daily Alert, the official public propaganda organ of the *Presidents of the Major American Jewish Organizations,* from May 31st to June 2, 2010 published every scurrilous Israeli state lie about the Israeli commandos being 'lynched' and 'attacked', and the human rights victims being responsible for the death of their comrades ... *not* the Israeli commandos. Not a single deviation, not a single word of criticism. Not even a single mention of even the superficial Israeli critics who faulted the execution, the use of deadly weapons, the assault in international waters, and the public relations fiasco. The vast majority of Israeli Jews and organized Zionists in the US supported the bloody massacre and were opposed by a small minority who has no access to the mass media. Zionist control over the mass media was once again demonstrated by the reporting through "Israel's eyes".[6] Essentially *The New York Times*, the *Washington Post*, CNN, CBS, and NBC presented the Israeli commandos attacking the humanitarian boat as being ... "assaulted and beaten".[7] *The New York Times* gave credence to the Israeli claim that its act of piracy on the high seas was *legal*.[8] For the US mass media the problem is not Israeli state terror, but how to *manipulate and disarm the outrage* of the international community. To that end the entire Zionist Power configuration has a reliable ally in the Zionized Obama White House and US Congress.

The Obama Response to Israeli State Terror

There is only one basic reason why Israel repeatedly commits crimes against humanity, including the latest assault on the humanitarian flotilla: because it knows that the Zionist Power Configuration, embedded in the US power structure, will ensure government support, in this case the Obama White House.

In the face of the world-wide condemnation of Israel's crime on the high seas, and calls from the international community for legal action, the Obama regime absolutely refused to criticize Israel. A White House spokesman said "*The United States deeply regrets the loss of life and injuries sustained and is currently working to understand the circumstances surrounding the tragedy*".[9] An act of state terrorism does not evoke "regrets"—it normally provokes condemnation and punishment. The power which caused "*loss of life and injuries*" has a name—Israel; the persons who suffered death and injuries during the Israeli assault—have a name—humanitarian volunteers. It was not simply a "loss of life" but a well planned premeditated murder which are openly defended by Prime Minister Netanyahu and his entire Cabinet. The "circumstances" of the murders are clear: Israel assaulted an unarmed ship in international waters, opening fire as they boarded the ship. The Obama regime's obscene political cover-up of a deliberate criminal act in violation of international law is evident in his description of a serial homicide as a '*tragedy*'. Premeditated state terror has no resemblance to a tragic noble ruler forced by circumstances into a criminal act against their closest allies.

Washington, pressed to participate at a UN Security Council meeting, spent 10 hours eliminating all references to Israel's illegal criminal act, ending in a resolution which merely calls for an "impartial" investigation, with Washington pushing for an Israeli investigatory committee. To the world at large, including the Turkish government, the Obama regime and the US government, by refusing to condemn Israel, are "*accomplices to a mass murder*".

To understand why the Obama regime brought shame and infamy to itself in the eyes of the world, one need look at the Zionist composition of the Obama White House and, equally important, the direct power and access that the principle Jewish-Zionist organizations have over the US political system. In the week preceding Israel's announced assault on the humanitarian flotilla, (pro-Israel) Jewish leaders met with over a third of US senators to pressure them to pass harsher sanctions on Iran by June. Among the key operatives attending were the Jewish Federation of North America, AIPAC and the rest of the Israeli Fifth Column.[10] The following day a squadron of leaders from the Jewish Federations flew into Washington to meet with top Obama administration officials, to ensure that the White House and Congress did not in any way or form publicly express any criticism of Israel's settlement policy. No doubt the Zionist apologists for Israeli war crimes extended their agenda to include no public criticism of the Israeli assault on the flotilla. Rahm Emmanuel, top US Presidential aide, was in Tel Aviv as a guest of top officials of the Israel Defense Force a few days before the IDF launched the assault, no doubt having filled Rahm in on the details. The Israeli-American aide to Obama no doubt assured the war criminals of Washington's unconditional political and military support for Israel's acts of aggression.

From within the Obama Administration and without, the aggressive pressure from the 51 principle organizations of the American Zionists have guaranteed Israeli war criminals *immunity* from any War Crimes Tribunal, or even serious political condemnation by the UN Security Council. The Zionized White House's tactic is to deflect attention from immediate consequential condemnation let alone sanctions, hoping that over time, aided by the blanket mass media apology in the US, the mass indignation and protest overseas will gradually wither away. Obama and his Zionist cohort are already in a belly crawl mode with Israel. Part of Rahm's mission to Israel was to hand Netanyahu an invitation to the White House, during the week of the slaughter at sea. The only reason Netanyahu did not come to Washington was because he rushed back to Israel to buttress the Foreign Office's defense of the slaughter in the face of world-wide outrage. But in a phone conversation, Obama promised Netanyahu a prompt new invitation—assuring the Israeli ringleader that violating international laws and bloodying dozens of humanitarian activists is of no consequence, especially since it insures continued financial support by Obama's Zionist backers.

Like Lyndon Johnson with the cover-up of the U.S.S. *Liberty,* Obama's apology of Israel's war crimes, is the price for ensuring the backing of billionaire Zionist financiers and media moguls, the tens of thousands of pro-Israel Jews and the 51 President of the Major American Jewish Organizations.

In the face of Washington's complicity with Israeli war crimes, the only road is to intensify the worldwide boycott, divestment and sanctions campaign against all Israeli products, cultural activities and professional exchanges. Hopefully, the Islamic led mass protests will find echo in the wider anti-Zionist Christian and Jewish communities—especially, when Israeli apologists for state terror make public appearances. Even more important each and every Israeli involved in the mass assault should be subject to criminal prosecution wherever they visit. Only by making the Israelis understand that they will pay a high price for their serial homicides and violations of international law will reason possibly enter their political narrative. Only by moving beyond symbolic protests, like recalling diplomats, and taking substantive actions, like breaking relations, will the international community isolate the perpetrator of state terrorism. All Americans should send a message loud and clear to President Obama—*NEVER AGAIN.* Otherwise, with the Zionist Power Configuration active 7/24, the Obama regime, true to the Zionist agenda, will once again focus attention on attacking Iran. Israel's action today with US complicity is a prelude to the kind of deadly force it has in store for sabotaging the recent Turkey-Brazil-Iran diplomatic agreement.

This is dedicated to the brave Turkish martyrs on the Mavi Marmara, May 31, 2010, and to the 34 murdered American sailors on the USS Liberty, June 8, 1967—all victims of an unrepentant criminal state—Israel.

Endnotes

1   *Financial Times*, June 2, 2010, p. 2.
2   "Israeli Soldiers Met by Well-Planned Lynch Mob", *Jerusalem Post*,
        March 31, 2010; "Israeli Soldiers Attacked", *IDF*, March 31, 2010.
3   *Ha'aretz*, May 30, 2010.
4   *Financial Times*, June 2, 2010, p. 2.
5   *Ynet News*, June 1, 2010.
6   FAIR, June 1, 2010.
7   *Washington Post*, June 1, 2010.
8   *The New York Times*, June 1, 2010.
9   AFP, May 31, 2010.
10   *Jewish Telegraph Agency*, May 26, 2010.

Made in United States
Orlando, FL
05 May 2024

46529923R00075